" It has become painfully obvious we have a need for strong father figures in our families. It's heartening to know that family values and fatherhood can and should still receive a prominent place in our society."
— **Congressman Wally Herger, 2nd District, CA**

"A heart-warming story of love and devotion of a dedicated father and a courageous son who overcame seemingly insurmountable odds."
— **Congressman Joseph R. Pitts, 18th District, PA**

"I enjoyed *Father, Son, 3-Mile Run* tremendously. I am going to require that all the young men in my program read this book. I consider it that important. Within the pages of this book, you find the ingredients of successful parenting and of loving and caring spiritual growth.
"I believe this book is greatly needed. Judge Leenhouts' love and commitment as a father should be an example for every father in our nation. His insight as a parent should be set in a blueprint for all men to follow. His book was truly an inspiration and an emotional and spiritual uplift for me personally."
— **Frank M. Victorio, Director, Moral Values Program**

"This updated version of the original book now simply entitled, *Father, Son, 3-Mile Run,* brings us new hope as it places the true meaning of life back into focus upon which all success is built...the family. Whether you are a father or son, or mother or daughter, white collar worker, blue collar worker, housewife or professional, this book will bring you a sense of new hope in a world which seems to be filled with continuous uncertainty."
— **F. Gerald Dash, Executive Director,**
Volunteers in Prevention, Probation & Prisons, Inc.

"I'm sorry that *Father, Son, 3-Mile Run* was not found by me when I was raising my sons. In these days, when so many youngsters are faced with making choices at an early age about alcohol and other drugs, gangs, and violence, there is a real need for more men to become mentors to boys who have no fathers. This book should inspire all men to become better fathers to their own sons and to any young man in need of guidance."
— **Marv Steinberg, Just Say No/Youth Power Clubs**

"*Father, Son, 3-Mile Run* is a wonderful book that is nothing less than inspirational. If the reader pays close attention he will discover that the principles and philosophies at work in the relationship between the author and his sons are not unlike those at work between us and our heavenly Father.

"I think every son, father, and grandfather who reads this book will surely benefit."
— Fred Lucero, Sr., TAC Officer, Shasta County Probation Dept.

"I especially was inspired by the fuller meaning of fatherhood. We desperately need men to take up the challenge to be fathers to their own children and to those who don't have one."
— K.C. Farrar, Executive Director, PlusONE Mentors, Inc.

"I was fortunate to have *Father, Son, 3-Mile Run* when raising my own sons, and I am delighted that it will be available to my grandsons."
— V. Robert Payant, President, The National Judicial College

"*Father, Son, 3-Mile Run* is a thought-provoking and sensitive book about responsible parenting of a father with his son. In our society, at this moment in time, there is an urgent need to learn the lessons the author so clearly articulates."
— Rev. William Stegall, United Methodist Church, Redding, CA

"Keith Leenhouts offers a virtuous life that we are both able to admire as well as strive to emulate. He so clearly lived and demonstrated a Christ-like love for his family and people of all ages and classes. Youth and parents would do well to read this book together."
— Tony Schultz, Pastor, Grace Lutheran Church, Ashland, OR

"Indeed, few things are more important to our society than fathers 'loving their children's mother.' Listening with our hearts, being present in love, having the message of our own Saviour, Jesus Christ, and the milk of human kindness and decency, will serve to change lives. Indeed, as Judge Leenhouts says, it is people that change people, not laws or regulations."
— Rev. Michael F. Kiernan, Sacred Heart Parish, Anderson, CA

Father, Son, 3-Mile Run

The Essence of Fatherhood

Keith J. Leenhouts

Clearwood Publishers   Bella Vista, California

FATHER, SON, 3-MILE RUN:
THE ESSENCE OF FATHERHOOD

© 1999 BY KEITH LEENHOUTS

CLEARWOOD PUBLISHERS
P.O. BOX 52
BELLA VISTA, CALIFORNIA
96008

Revised Edition, 1999
Printed in Canada

Library of Congress Card Catalog Number: 98-73297
ISBN 0-9649997-4-9

Scripture quotations are from the Revised Standard Version
of the Bible, copyright 1946, 1952, 1971 and 1973 by the
Division of Christian Education, National Council of Churches

COVER: Andrew Morris, cross-country runner
COVER PHOTO: Bill Joseph, coach, Redding, CA
COVER DESIGN: George Foster, Fairfield, IA

Dedicated to the furtherance of fatherhood...

FATHER, SON,
3-MILE RUN

FOREWORD

"Where have all the fathers gone? Why do we put so many tasks before fatherhood? Why do we spend time around the house, at our jobs, at our golf games, at everything but fatherhood?"…Keith Leenhouts.

The above quote, taken from the pages that follow, reminds me of a popular song in the 1960's, a time when scenes from the bloody police action in Vietnam filled television screens every evening during the news hour. A time when we dined to full color footage of incredible brutality. The rat-a-tat-tat of friendly or enemy fire punctuated blessings offered and "Amens" before we lifted knives and forks to begin a meal. It was a time when body counts instead of baseball stats ruled. The popular protest song of the day, *Where Have All the Flowers Gone?* played through the hearts of families bereft of their soldier sons. As the body counts grew, so did the tension in our society. Tempers flared. Families were split in two. Our nation began to come apart. Something had to be done. The war was affecting everyone. I experienced these things all too well—my husband, Al Doiron, died from wounds he received in those bloody jungles of Vietnam.

Now we approach the end of the millenium. On a dozen or more action-packed *Top Cops*-style shows, at varying hours of the day, including dinner time, we, the TV viewing public, witness and absorb the police action taking place in our country's major cities; often in our own communities; sometimes right next door.

1996 statistics revealed Washington D.C. had six times the per capita murder rate of the next highest state and sixty times that of Japan. Comparable statistics are not available for domestic violence and abuse, but preliminary studies indicate

American women and children are subjected to violence, abuse, and neglect as never before seen or imagined here or around the world. Over ten percent of our nation's women are abused by their male partners each year. 1997 estimates suggest that one out of three women and one out of six men suffered sexual molestation as a child.

Out of the Vietnam era, death and/or mayhem at the hands of one's own troops earned the term friendly fire. If we believe statistics, if we believe the investigative reporters' videotapes, the on-screen, hair-pulling battles between family members broadcast daily to millions of living rooms—then we are a nation at war with ourselves. Unable to ascertain body counts, the number of bruised, crippled, impaired, murdered—by friendly fire—mounts up.

"Where have all the fathers gone? Long time passing …gone to flowers every one. When will they ever learn? When will they e—ver learn?"

Different lyrics apply to our times, creating a cycle wherein fathers, rather than flowers, are missed; wherein young men become felons, go to prisons, go to graveyards...every one. When will "we" ever learn? When?

How much human carnage will it take before we as a community, a nation, recognize our desperate need to stop the cycle? Repair the wounded? Bring bona fide husbands and fathers—men who desire to love and nurture their wives and children—back into our midst?

Today we look out upon a vast population of broken families, children bereft of their fathers. Fathers who continue to sleep in the same house but fail to nurture their wives and children—some handing out beatings rather than hugs; some offering chilly silence rather than love; some absented to a golf course or local pub to rub elbows with their buddies rather than toss a ball back-and-forth in the yard with some little guy who can't get it right. When will we e—ver learn?

A Father, A Son, And A Three-Mile Run was written

twenty-five years ago as a gift from a father to his son. The message of the book proved so powerful, it was picked up by a publishing house and widely distributed. An inspirational movie based on the book was later produced and shown at numerous churches and family retreats.

Larry Boisclaire, the current publisher of this timeless gem, first encountered the book in 1978. He bought more than a hundred copies, passing them out over the years to young fathers—young fathers who, like himself, hungered for inspiration and instruction in the challenging task of fathering. While attempting to replenish his supply in 1997, he learned the book was out of print. Boisclaire contacted the author, Keith Leenhouts, who granted publication rights to Larry and Yvonne Boisclaire, so that they might resurrect *A Father, A Son, A Three-Mile Run*. Now, as the publishers, the Boisclaires hope to again spread this inspiring story. Today, the messages contained are even more urgent for the hectic homelife of single parents or two working spouses and latchkey kids. The messages are timeless, offering the most powerful weapon since the dawn of family—the love of a father for his child, wife, and fellow man.

This revised edition of *Father, Son, 3-Mile Run* drops the "A's" from the original title. Why? Because Keith Leenhouts produced a book embracing more than his own particular father-son relationship—one that wraps its arms around the essence of Father, of Son, of the distance in time and hard work one generation must travel to nurture the next. This book is not just for or about fathers. *Father, Son, 3-Mile Run* is for anyone who aspires towards nobleness of spirit, of action, and loving human behavior. May you savor the truth about the power of love within these pages, and may it become manifested in your life as it is in the person of Keith Leenhouts.

Lynn Doiron, Contributing author of
  I've Always Meant to Tell You: Letters to Our Mothers

CONTENTS

ACKNOWLEDGMENTS

Forces of love or forces of fear motivate our actions and program our responses. An abundance of the former and a trifle of the latter have blessed me. The Apostle John wrote that perfect love casts out all fear. I am grateful to the triune God for the many ways He has revealed His love for me and for His inspiration in my life. For without His love I would be but a clanging cymbal.

My parents, my wife, Audrey, and my three sons, Bill, Dave, and Jim, have been constants in my life. Their love and support, freely given, has strengthened and encouraged me throughout my life.

My church family, my friends and colleagues, and the citizens of Royal Oak, Michigan, have been a continual source of inestimable blessing.

Those who purchased previous editions of the book and wrote letters of appreciation have been an immense source of encouraging energy. A special thanks to Larry and Yvonne Boisclaire with Clearwood Publishers, and to their editor, Lynn Doiron, for making possible the continued ministry of *Father, Son, 3-Mile Run.*

Keith Leenhouts

1 From the Ashes of Defeat

One hundred and forty runners crowded the long starting line. Most hadn't slept much the night before. All woke up early. Pre-race muscles stretched taut over their lean frames. Some touched their toes. Others cricked their necks and bent side to side at the waist. A few extended one leg forward, then switched and stretched the opposite leg in similar fashion. Maybe stretching would help to release the buildup of anticipative tension.

The normally bright and smiling youthful faces appeared drawn and serious as each harrier contemplated what lay ahead—the grueling three-mile cross-country race against the best high school runners in the state. All were dedicated athletes who had run between five and fifteen miles every day for most of their high school years in preparation for this climactic moment: the 1972 Michigan High School Cross-Country Championship. To come this far, these runners had beaten thousands of competitors in a series of state-wide regional high school meets. Now they crouched in starting positions, every nerve ending tuned for the imminent "Crack!" of the starter's pistol.

For one gangly youth of medium height named Bill, and for me, his gray-templed father, the significance of this race reached far beyond the pursuit of athletic victory. This was a race made possible by love—an uncommon love relationship that perhaps belonged to past generations, not our present society of rejected children, rejected parents, and rejected values.

I looked at Bill tensed at the starting line. The rounded features of his face seemed chiseled, perhaps by expectation and fear. I knew that for the next three miles he would not only battle Michigan's best high school runners, but also a lifetime of academic and physical setbacks.

Cross-country is among the most demanding of sports. It is uplifting to talk to football and basketball players and tell them your son is in cross-country, then listen to the heroes of the glamour sports say, "Man, that really takes guts. I could never do that."

Cross-country requires an exceptional combination of speed and stamina to run flat-out for several miles across native terrain. The narrow trail twists and climbs exposing obstacles and the unexpected: loose footing, roots, and bunched groups of competitive runners.

The excited noise of the crowd stilled to a hushed silence as the starter raised his gun. I wondered if this, Bill's final high school race, would end in a long-awaited victory.

2 Overcoming

Crack! A rainbow of seven-man groups, clad in colored T-shirts and shorts, burst from the line. "Crack! Crack!" Two more shots split the cold, crisp November air, signaling a false start. Two runners had started before the gun was fired.

"All right, men, relax a little. You've got a long way to go," said the starter, a soft-spoken, grandfatherly gentleman. The *thinclads*, many already glistening with sweat, jogged back to the starting line, flapping their arms and loosening up their legs to prevent sudden incapacitating leg cramps.

Bill looked pale and nervous as the runners regrouped at the line. *Does he really belong here?* I wondered. *Certainly most of the other runners are endowed with greater strength and speed. Measurements can be made in feet, inches, and miles per hour, but has anyone invented a scale to measure the strength of young man's heart?*

Impossible. Over the years victory for Bill had been illusive, often out of reach. Our son had learned, along with his mother, Audrey, and me, to accept his defeats as a challenge for improvement.

For years Bill ran under the shadow of defeats. His recent streak of victories included a distant yet qualifying eighth place finish in the regionals. His successful turnabout garnered him a coveted position on this starting line.

By comparing his time with the other competitors, he should, theoretically, finish below seventieth place. But only the top fifteen would attain All-State status. Would inner desire make a difference? Could it carry him to his sought after All-State goal?

In his eighteen years Bill had suffered many setbacks. Grade school had been a relentless series of trials. Though he tried hard, six-year-old Bill could not grasp first-grade reading fundamentals. The importance of good reading skills was not lost on Audrey or me. After talking it over with Bill and his teacher, we agreed Bill should repeat first grade.

Bill did not complain about this decision. He met the challenge by working harder. Still, younger classmates surpassed him in their ability to learn. As children will do, they added to Bill's burden by ridiculing him for flunking.

By third grade Bill's teacher had branded him a failure and cast him on the academic dump heap. She called Audrey and me into her office for the first of what proved to be many conferences. We went with apprehension and concern. Had Bill misbehaved? Wasn't he trying? Didn't he care about school anymore?

After a few minutes of polite small talk, his teacher, a plump, bespectacled, stern-looking woman, came to the point. "I'm afraid I have some very unpleasant news for you, Judge and Mrs. Leenhouts." Voice lowered, she said, "Your son Bill will never be able to attend college. He just does not have the mental ability." She held our attention with her obvious concern, glancing from Audrey to me between pauses. "Certainly," she continued, "he tries. And no child is more lovable. But he just can't achieve...academically. I'm very sorry to have to tell you this. I know it must be a terrible shock."

I leaned back against the stiff slats of the wooden chair until they creaked with my weight, breathed deeply, and said in a sigh of relief, "Is that all? We were afraid you had some really dreadful news for us."

The furrowed lines of her brow appeared to melt as her eyes widened in what seemed to be bewilderment, then disbelief. "Isn't it important to you that your son goes to college? Don't you feel he must?" she stammered. "After all, you're the judge of our city. What will people think if the judge's son doesn't go to college? Won't you be embarrassed?"

Audrey and I exchanged a glance. We both realized that the teacher's concern had somehow become misplaced—directed toward me rather than her student. I noticed a thin line of perspiration above her upper lip and suppressed a laugh of relief as I explained that my ego did not need feeding by a son who went to college. "Neither my wife nor I are concerned that our son's academic shortcomings will diminish my reputation." Audrey squeezed my hand as I continued, "We hope Bill will attend college someday for his sake. More importantly, though, we want him to grow up with a love for the Lord and his fellowman and always give his personal best at whatever he tries."

Three years later Bill's sixth-grade teacher called us in. She said, "Judge and Mrs. Leenhouts, I'm sorry to have to tell you this, but Bill is no longer trying—he has given up completely. I'm not surprised. In fact, after talking with his other teachers, I'm more amazed that he didn't give up long ago. We have all observed the same efforts and failures and wondered how long this determined little boy could maintain such tremendous desire. How long he could keep trying. He has little to show for years of hard work. Now he's given up." She looked away from us for a moment to add, "No one can blame him."

When her gaze returned to us, it seemed obvious that she shared our greatest fear: that Bill might have lost forever a good image about himself—that precious but fragile self-esteem that could tip the balance toward success and away from failure later in life.

I was grieved by her words. At that moment I fully understood just how much our Bill had suffered. I also knew the humiliation of prolonged failure. I had endured that same struggle as the slowest learner throughout my grade school years.

That night, when Bill and I had our private moments together at bedtime, I revealed my own grade school experiences. I told him that some thirty years before, I had been labeled the dumbest kid in my class. "With the help, love, and understanding of my mother, father, and teachers, I stumbled through those years," I told him, adding with a shrug, "Even law school. But just look at me now. A judge!"

As I left Bill's bedroom after our nighttime prayers, I turned to him and said, "Bill, I know that someday, someway, you will become the greatest of the Leenhouts."

"You know, Dad," he answered, "I guess that not doing so good isn't all that bad if someone loves you and stands by you." I knew in that moment a glimmer of hope still existed; contrary to all his teachers' beliefs and observations, and in the face of so many defeats, our son would continue to try.

It took nearly two years for us to confirm the suspicion that Bill suffered impaired vision. Finally, an expert diagnosed the problem as a paralyzed muscle in his left eye. The resulting double vision improved with the help of the eye specialist, who developed perceptual, tactile, and motor coordination exercises to correct the problem.

Progress moved forward at a snail's pace, but Bill continued to give his maximum effort. Each night after dinner Audrey or I would accompany him to the basement. There, free of distractions, his eyes tracked a ball swinging from side to side on a string or the path of our fingers tracing around a coat hanger bent in a circle. Then he would seclude himself in his upstairs bedroom and study, study, study until bedtime. The doctor was impressed by Bill's determination to overcome his handicap.

To everyone's surprise Bill made honor roll throughout junior high school and continued to maintain just under a B average as a senior. Just as his academic achievements resulted from hard work and desire—not natural ability—so, too, did his success in athletics. He reached deep inside for that miraculous strength—desire of the heart—to propel himself past defeat and on to victory.

Bill's first attempts at football, baseball, and track were every bit as unsuccessful as his early academic performance. I must admit that he came by his physical shortcomings honestly. During my school years, I, too, was a non-achieving athlete. But despite our limited talent, both Bill and I loved to participate in sports.

Since I love kids, and since I enjoy their companionship, I volunteered to coach Bill's flag football team at the first opportunity. Young boys who choose to play football in our city, Royal Oak, Michigan, can play in either of two leagues. Those who are gifted athletically usually elect to sign up for Little League football. The teams in this division play tough, serious ball with an emphasis on winning.

The less athletically inclined boys opt for flag football, a toned-down version of the game, which resembles touch football more than tackle. Each player inserts a small flag under his belt. Instead of using brute force, the ball carrier is downed by pulling off his flag. The predominant philosophy in this league is simple: "Let everyone play and have fun."

When Bill was eight we joined the lesser athletes—these were our kind of kids. We felt at home.

As the coach I was determined to let every boy on our team play every game. I hoped these kids might gain a feeling of accomplishment and develop a good self-image. It didn't matter if we won or lost. In fact, I hoped we might lose some games so the boys would learn how to handle defeat as well as victory.

Much to our surprise we won every game that first year—often by a big score. Several boys on our team were fast and skillful enough to have played in the Little League division. Yet they chose to play with us. We couldn't lose, even though I shuffled the boys around to every position.

And Bill? He was, well, ineffectual. Most of the time he didn't know or care which way we were running the ball or even who had won. At the end of the game, I would feel an inner hurt as this skinny, dirty little boy shuffled off the field and watched his teammates run off together for an afternoon of play. When he reached me he would look up, smile, and reach out his hand, and we would leave for our customary Saturday afternoon together.

Mainly to please me, I suppose, Bill stuck with flag football. For four years I played him at center where he could be of the most help and the least harm. I told him he was the center because he was the one guy I could rely upon to begin the play by hiking the ball to the correct player. Thus, little by little, Bill gained a sense of accomplishment.

We all need to succeed at something and feel good

about ourselves. When we are underachievers, someone has to love us enough to convince us we have made a contribution. Without knowing it, I had learned this lesson thirty years earlier when I was in sixth grade.

Being the slowest learner in class, I had a deplorable self-image. I didn't think I was then, or ever would be, good for anything. But my sixth-grade teacher understood. More importantly, she loved me. She made sure I was one of the boys chosen to be a corner crossing guard. Me, a crossing guard! I was good for something after all. Someone had made me feel needed. I tried to do the same for our son.

Bill dutifully played every game, believing he was the most important boy on the team. During the last year he finally experienced a bona fide triumph. He intercepted a pass and ran it back for a touchdown. It was a small feat, perhaps, compared with the accomplishments of other players. Nonetheless, this moment belonged to him.

In the spring of Bill's first year of junior high, he tried out for the school baseball team. Bill trained hard and never missed a practice. But, for the coach, winning was the major consideration. He let Bill play in only two games—in the late innings and in right field where the opposing hitters were least likely to hit the ball. The coach didn't let him bat, not once, all year.

I often wonder if the coach, the players, the students, the fans—or anyone else who had anything to do with the team of thirteen and fourteen-year-old boys—now remember the won-lost record for that year. Somebody must remember. It was so important for the team to win, that one kid, who never missed a practice, was not given a single opportunity to step up to the plate and swing his bat.

Some adults wonder why many youths grow up with

a distorted set of values. It's no mystery. Such youngsters learn early that victory, championships, prestige, and outward show are among the most important values of adult life.

A nearby high school athletic team, for example, had won 90 percent of their games for three consecutive years. The local press raved over the team's success. Yet some of us considered it one of the city's most unsuccessful sports programs. Only fifteen young men out of each class of eight hundred students got to play. The competition for a position on the team was fierce. Many freshmen boys cut from the team threw their spikes in disgust into a dark basement corner, never to pick them up again.

In contrast, another high school team in the area cut no one from the freshman and sophomore teams. This team struggled to win any games, let alone a championship. Yet every boy played. Any youth willing to practice faithfully and work hard experienced the thrill of making the varsity team. Over the years hundreds of young men benefited. They have experienced personal success, achievement, and positive self-esteem. This resulted because of the unique philosophy of an inspirational coach. Overall growth of individual players counted, not the fleeting goal of winning.

Bill decided he didn't care to try out again for a sport where so much emphasis was placed on the team's won-lost record. A sport where, no matter how hard he worked, he probably wouldn't get a chance at bat. So he went out for track in the eighth grade, a sport in which no one is cut from the team.

Bill lost every race he ran during his first track season, usually by a considerable margin. With every loss Bill grew more determined and trained harder at improving his time.

Defeat didn't slow him down. He had suffered so many setbacks in his life, another string of defeats wasn't devastating to him.

One of Bill's friends, a boy who had been the fastest runner in our flag football league, also went out for track in junior high school. He won every race that year with ease. The second year he lost a few races. Then, during his junior year, he lost more often than he won. Dejected, he quit the team. Easy victories early on had paved the way for his ultimate defeat.

Bill kept running. He ran with the freshman cross-country team the next fall and consistently finished, although failing, with equal consistency, to place. At the close of the season, Royal Oak's two high schools held a freshman meet. As always Bill ran as fast as he possibly could. Near the end of the race, he was in fifth place, about a quarter mile behind the leader. Suddenly, another runner challenged Bill. As he came alongside, his elbow caught Bill, nearly knocking him from the path.

Bill reacted aggressively—he pushed back, ran harder, and held on to finish fifth. He had never before displayed that kind of competitiveness. He hadn't cared who won our flag football games. He had never before struck back when he was pushed. His attitude toward aggressive athletes had been, "If winning is that important to you, go ahead. I really don't care one way or the other."

The following winter months were filled with hope and encouragement as our talks together dwelled on one subject—not Bill's distant fifth-place finish out of eight runners, but his new spirit of competitiveness.

The cross-country team's captain and top runner, Phil Ceeley, had also taken notice. Phil would later receive the Kimball High School trophy for outstanding achievement in athletics and academics. He showed Bill his training courses—the five, ten, and fifteen-mile routes he had used to develop the toughness and endurance that helped him win All-State. Phil's well-beaten paths became Bill's. And earning All-State honors became Bill's goal.

Bill worked tirelessly at attaining that goal. He became a familiar figure on Royal Oak's streets, running five to fifteen miles a day, every day, through the snow, sleet, and bitter cold of winter; the driving rains of spring; the sultry heat of summer.

A statement uttered by Jim Ryun, the world-class miler from Kansas, encouraged Bill during the dead of winter. "It seems strange," Ryun said, "but I think the cold winters of Kansas gave me the toughness that I needed."

To relieve the monotony of seeing the same streets over and over, Bill tacked up a map of the United States on the basement wall and imagined himself running west across the country. Periodically, he would draw a line along the highways to record the miles he had run. After three years of running, the black line wove its way from Detroit to Los Angeles and halfway back.

Bill continued to lose almost every race he ran until his senior year. Then his desire and thousands of miles of hard training began to pay off. The long progression of defeats eased to a close when his teammates elected him co-captain. Bill had become his team's fastest runner.

Still, his goal of being All-State seemed unattainable. To achieve this dream he would have to beat thousands of runners, most of whom were blessed with superior natural athletic ability. *Impossible*, I had thought. Then Bill and his team qualified at the regional meet.

I let my gaze drift from Bill to the other Royal Oak runners at the starting line. Had each of these youths overcome odds against winning comparable to Bill's? *Impossible*, still echoed through my thoughts, my being. *Bill had conquered so many obstacles. Now this one last chance beckoned him. Could he achieve his goal? Bill had climbed much farther than the others to reach this pinnacle—he would have a greater distance to fall.*

Bill and I had talked about the challenge of the impossible as demonstrated in the life of Glenn Cunningham, the great miler of the 1930's. As a small boy Glenn was severely burned when he and his brother were building a fire in the schoolhouse furnace. For many days it looked as if his mutilated legs would have to be amputated. But Glenn begged and pleaded so strongly that his parents postponed the imminent amputation. The doctors adamantly proclaimed that Glenn would never run again. He would be lucky to even walk.

Days, months, and years of torturous effort followed. First came that day of standing momentarily and collapsing back into bed; then the first step; finally, a second and a third. One day he walked again on legs that, according to doctors, simply could not hold his weight. Further progress came: his first awkward strides at jogging, followed by running.

In time Glenn Cunningham—despite scar tissue, a lack of arch support, and missing toes—began to win races in high school. He went on to college and eventually set a world record for the mile in 1934. Other runners have come along who have beaten Cunningham's time. None, however, have surpassed his legacy of courage and just plain guts.

3 Father-Son Beginnings

Crack! The starter's gun again signaled the beginning of the intense sixteen-minute drama. No false start. No second shot. This was it. They were underway.

Bill and his rivals began their arduous three-mile journey over hills, through forests, and cross-country. My heart pulsed in my neck; my legs seemed about to buckle. Bill appeared hemmed in by the others, a disadvantage in racing. A husky voice left my throat, and the chilly November air carried my shouts of "Go Billy Blue!" to our son who wore the blue of Royal Oak Kimball High School.

I hurried along with some of the other spectators to a flat one-hundred-fifty-yard stretch at the bottom of a hill near the quarter-mile mark. From there we could catch our next glimpse of the runners. My forty-seven-year-old legs would not move as fast as I wanted them to, but I reached the vantage point as the first runner burst into view. I strained my eyes. Though I could not make out his face, I could tell by the runner's style that he was not Bill.

Every runner has his distinct way of running—a style evolved from his physical attributes and sharpened by his coaches. In similar fashion, wise fathers don't try to recreate their sons into their own images. Instead, they assist their sons in sharpening their God-given gifts and talents by providing encouragement, instruction, and guidance.

W henever I meet a new father, aglow with biological triumph, I get the urge to say, "Just wait. There's more to being a father than you think." But I refrain from saying it. He may turn out to be one of those fellows with a natural instinct for fatherhood—a talent that I have concluded is as rare as the perfect pitch. For most of us, fatherhood, like everything else worthwhile, requires lots of hard work. True, it is a labor of love, but hard work nonetheless.

Me, a father? Incredible, I thought to myself after my bride of a few months whispered into my ear, "I think we're going to have a baby." Bursting with pride, I must have stood in front of the mirror for fifteen minutes the next morning, congratulating the beaming face that grinned back at me. *Wow, I did it. I didn't know I had it in me.*

Months flashed by. Then our first baby was born premature on an unusually cold Fourth of July weekend. In no time my wife's pain and my concern gave way to relief—two arms, two legs, enough fingers and toes—then to joy. A son. What an extraordinary gift, especially for an ordinary guy like me.

My exhausted Audrey, pale as the sheets she lay upon, looked more beautiful than ever. At that moment our whole existence was rolled up into one helpless little six-pound bundle of life.

The big day came when I brought them home to our small apartment and Audrey handed our son to me to carry upstairs. I wasn't prepared for her request and gave her an anxious, "Couldn't you do it?" look. But she shook her head and said, to reassure me and perhaps herself, "Don't be afraid of him, silly, he won't break."

My shaking hands clutched the blue blanket with Bill's squirming body swaddled inside. At that moment I suspected that fatherhood, rather than being one uninterrupted joy after another, was more likely to be a series of duties.

One morning a few days later, long before I was ready to rise, my suspicions were confirmed. Bill started to cry. It was feeding time. I thought Audrey must have overslept, so I turned over and closed my eyes. The wailing from the living room nursery went up a decibel or two. My wife was faking, I decided. But I couldn't just roll over and shout, "Go feed our child." She might reply, "Why don't you?" Then what would I say?

I puzzled about it while the crying continued, until I realized that if Audrey was faking she wouldn't admit it. This permitted me to get up and feed Bill without establishing a precedent.

Fumbling around like the sorcerer's apprentice, I sterilized, measured, and capped bottles amidst great clouds of steam. I tried unsuccessfully to quiet Bill while the bottle warmed. The nipple clogged shut, the bottle got too hot, and there seemed to be no comfortable way to hold him. Finally, we reached equilibrium and he sucked away.

I confess I felt a certain pride in eliciting a hearty burp from him when the operation was over. Yet I looked upon the whole affair as an immense obligation I wished never need be repeated—a wish that was not to be granted.

I made the decision early on to put a high priority on fatherhood. Although this was an easy decision for me to make, I had to learn what to do in order to be effective. Only a patient wife and a trio of charitable sons turned me into any kind of parent at all.

Parental obligations grew right along with Bill. Shortly after his fourth birthday, I was pressed into service as a disciplinarian. I had aspired to be—as Carl Sandburg expressed of Lincoln—"Both steel and velvet, who is as hard as rock and soft as drifting fog."* Unfortunately, my debut as a disciplinarian was a flop.

I was working in the garage. The little neighbor girl Bill had been playing with ran past the open door crying, "Billy hit me. Billy hit me." As a member of the old school, I believe you shouldn't hit girls no matter how great the provocation. I grabbed a nearby board to use as a paddle and rushed to the backyard. There, Bill, who seemed unaware of the dastardly deed he had just committed, maneuvered his toy dump truck while growling engine sounds. I hoisted him by his shirt collar and whacked his posterior with the makeshift paddle, at the same time administering a lecture about courtesy to females.

Bill ran wailing into the garage clutching the seat of his pants. At that same moment Audrey emerged from the house, arms folded tightly across her chest. "Why did you spank him?" She demanded. "Did you see what happened?"

"Well, uh, not exactly," I replied sheepishly, "But the neighbor girl said Bill hit her."

"That's a terrible way for a lawyer to act," she continued. "You punished Billy without finding out the facts. That little girl has been bothering him for a long time, and Billy kept trying to make her leave him alone. Finally, he pushed her

*Sandburg offered the explanation that Lincoln was hard in commanding a terrible civil war, in requiring conscription of soldiers for the first time in America, and for suspending the right of habeas corpus. Yet he was soft, as indicated by his letter to the widow Mrs. Bixby (21 November 1864) and by his commitment to the postwar South: "With malice toward none, with charity for all." These remarks were made by Sandburg before a Joint Session of Congress and the assembled diplomatic corps on 12 February 1959.

gently, just to let her know he didn't want her that close. He certainly didn't hit her. He really couldn't have handled the situation any better."

I shifted my eyes from my wife's cold glare. Searching for an inviting spot on the ground to stare at, I noticed the tip of a rusty nail sticking out of a board—the one which I had just used to swat Bill with. I rushed into the garage. Just as I feared, the nail had punctured the spot on Bill's derriere that he was rubbing. I couldn't believe what I'd done.

Half an hour later, after giving Bill a preventative tetanus shot, the doctor asked, "By the way, Keith, how did this happen?"

"I'd rather not talk about it," I replied. Fortunately, he was a friend who accepted my terse reply without question.

After that experience I decided never again to touch Bill in anger. As it turned out, I didn't have to. All I had to do was express disapproval by facial expression or words. That proved to be punishment enough.

Another year of duties, obligations, and sacrifices of fatherhood passed. Instead of frequenting Friday-night high school football games with my friends, Bill and I stood on the railroad tracks overlooking the gridiron. From that viewpoint I divided my time between watching the game and watching Bill build imaginary fires. I avoided staying up late on weekend nights so that I would have energy to play with Bill on Saturday and Sunday afternoons. Golf matches with friends were suspended.

I accepted all these sacrifices and more, not because I particularly wanted to but because I felt I should. My belief —that true happiness is found in the fulfillment of duties, not in the pursuit of joys—pacified any doubts regarding how I spent my free time.

Then on a bitterly cold January day when Bill was five, I made a profound discovery: *Fatherhood isn't just duties.*

Fatherhood is joy.

That entire Saturday afternoon I spent with Bill, teaching him how to ice skate. Our rink was a neighbor's frozen backyard swimming pool, and Bill's goal was to skate the full length. Each time Bill slipped and fell, I helped him to his feet. Finally, he made it—his red cheeks taut with determination and staccato puffs of steamy breath shooting through the wool scarf that covered his mouth. Well, I should say, part of him made it. Just before he reached the end of the pool, he tripped and smacked his nose on the edge.

"That was great!" I exclaimed, skating over to where he was struggling to stand. I picked him up and held him close. Rubbing his nose and looking at the bright red blood staining the snow in his mittens, he looked up at me through tears and sniffed, "I-I didn't think it was so great."

I began to laugh, but not so much because of what he had said and done. Suddenly, standing there on my ice skates, wiping blood from the nose of our five-year-old son, I realized I was with Bill because I loved him. Except for his mother, I would rather be with him than with anyone else in the entire world.

What a transcendent moment. I no longer felt that time spent with Bill meant giving up some other activity. A vision of my future emerged that included a new potential for loving. Fatherhood, no longer just a duty, blossomed that afternoon into one of the greatest experiences I would ever know.

My time of putting Bill to bed at night became a joy. Audrey had him all day. I wanted him for at least part of the evening. Each night we had fifteen minutes or so to ourselves behind closed doors. I came to look upon those fifteen minutes with Bill—and later with his two brothers—as the best part of my day.

We spent most of that time talking about a very important subject: nothing. We mentioned whatever happened to be at the top of our heads or hearts. Sometimes we talked about the best or worst things that had happened to us that day, or about exceptional men and women we knew. Gordie Howe, Al Kaline, and the University of Michigan football team were all subjects of our conversations. We finished our talks by telling Jesus stories and saying our prayers together.

One evening, typical of many during my ten years as a municipal court judge, a PTA mother called me at home. She requested that I speak at one of their meetings.

"How late can I come and still accommodate you?" I asked.

She replied, "You can speak at nine o'clock after we conduct our business meeting. Why? Do you have some other important business to attend to."

"Yes," I answered. "I'd like to put our sons to bed before I leave."

"You put your kids to bed?" she exclaimed in amazement. "I can't believe it. My husband has never put our kids to bed—not once. He's too busy reading his newspaper."

Her reply and the dozens of other similar statements I'd heard over the years bewildered me. I couldn't understand why so many fathers were preoccupied. Why couldn't they find enough time to participate in the lives of their sons and daughters?

Unfortunately, it wasn't simply a case of fathers shunning responsibilities they felt belonged to their wives; their indifference was further revealed by how few fathers joined their sons in sports activities. Our flag football team, for example, played every Saturday for three months. Out of twenty boys, two, perhaps three of their fathers attended games and only once or twice at that.

After a game in which two brothers played some real heads-up ball, I asked them—one a fast halfback and the other an end who caught most of our passes—where their dad was.

Their answer disturbed me: "Oh, he likes to sleep late on Saturday mornings. He's usually in bed until noon."

Another team member, Gary, was an average player who usually handed off to the faster runners during the game. But late in the fourth period of one very close contest, we called a special play. Gary faked a handoff, kept the ball, and ran sixty yards up the middle for a touchdown to tie the score. We held the other team on downs and got the ball again with only a few seconds to go. We called the same play, and Gary ran up the middle for a second touchdown. We won! Gary's teammates swarmed all over him. It was the kind of moment I wish every boy and his father could share at least once. But Gary's father wasn't there.

A few days later I saw Gary's father downtown and remarked about his son's game-winning touchdowns.

"Gee, that's funny," he said. "Gary didn't tell me about it. I wonder why?"

"Why weren't you at the game to witness his extraordinary feat?" I blurted.

"Uh, I had some work to do around the house," he replied.

Before I knew it, "Maybe if you had cared enough to watch your son play at least once during the season, he would have told you about his great moment," had slipped out.

Bill's youngest brother, Jim, played hockey. As I watched game after game, I noticed that most of the other fathers weren't there. I asked one friend why he didn't come to watch his son play, "Oh, I don't like hockey," he explained.

Doesn't he know that you don't go to your son's games to see hockey? I thought. *You go to watch your son. If you want to watch hockey, you go see the Detroit Red Wings play.*

Where have all the fathers gone? Why do we put so

many tasks before fatherhood? Why do we spend time around the house, at our jobs, at our golf games, at everything but fatherhood?

Perhaps our priorities have become jumbled because we've become unsure of our roles as fathers. We feel torn between family and career. Men are derided for their poor performance as husbands and fathers, yet how does American society define success? Too often, happiness and success are equated with the accumulation of consumer goods—capitalism flourishes this way. Time spent at work is considered more productive—hence more valuable—than time spent at home or on vacation with the family.

The ranks of absentee fathers increase year by year. No accidental lapse of fatherly responsibilities has spawned this epidemic. Divorce forces fathers away from their children. Rampant consumerism, burdensome taxes, and the high cost of living drive fathers to work long hours.

We are now witnessing the same phenomena with mothers. Government and industry-sponsored day care centers enthusiastically support the transition from home to the workplace. Women who stay home to care for their families are looked upon as relics of the past.

In choosing family life as their top priority, parents must buck the negative trend of society. There needn't be this conflict between children and work. Having both a career and family is possible. But marriage and child rearing require a major effort in order to be successful. Families need both quality and quantity time together. They need one another.

As a young father I traveled to St. Louis for a meeting. While there I visited a Methodist settlement house for underprivileged children. This visit, perhaps more than any other experience of my life, convinced me of the importance of spending time with children. I have handled many court cases reflecting child neglect in my years on the bench, but nothing could have prepared me for what I heard.

The house manager was a gray-haired Methodist minister who loved and helped many forgotten children—those who otherwise had no hope nor love. "We teach religion here," he said. "But we have to teach it quite a bit differently than what you might be used to. How many times have you heard it said, 'God is like a father' or 'God the Father'? Well, we can't tell these children that God is like a father. The kids here have been beaten, molested, sworn at, screamed at, and spit upon by their fathers—often alcoholics who, in time, desert them. If we tell these kids that God is like a father, they will have nothing to do with God.

"The sad fact is that each kid thinks he is at fault," the manager continued. "They often say to themselves or even out loud, 'Other kids have dads who don't beat them or leave them. What's wrong with me?' We know there is something wrong, of course—with the father, not the child. But the kids don't know that."

His words penetrated like a white-hot knife blade. If I had needed a motivating force, I now had one. I must strive at being a good father. Then, when Bill and his brothers heard that God is like a father, they would want to be with Him. The realization that my behavior as a father could cause them to shun God was appalling.

The father-son relationship Bill and I shared was not a one-sided affair with me doing the giving and Bill the receiving. Bill's influence on me was profound and far-reaching. His first effect on me was a new and full realization of what love and sacrifice means.

When Bill was just a baby, I often sacrificed my early

morning sleep. With eyelids still trying to slide shut, I would nestle into an over-stuffed armchair to feed our hungry infant son. In those moments, bathed in the soft, shadowy-red pre-dawn light, I began to fathom the unspoken, sometimes stern, fatherly love that had been poured into me as a child.

I was four when the Great Depression engulfed our country and fourteen when it ended. Most of my contemporaries still have intense, unpleasant memories of that era. Not I. Though my dad earned only $900 a year as a bank trust officer, he made me feel secure; I was never aware of the burdens and worries that must have nearly crushed his mind and spirit.

With the gift of awareness I received through Bill, I could freely express to my father how much I appreciated the sacrifices he had made for me. My father died when Bill was six months old, but not before I let him know how grateful I was for his loving care.

Bill had a healing, almost magical effect on me. As the responsibilities accompanying law practice, and later a judgeship, occupied my heart and mind, I came to appreciate him more and more. One night, as I pulled a thick, homemade quilt under his chin and tucked it around his tiny shoulders, I searched for a way to let him know how his magic soothed my life. A long-remembered poem came to mind, and I paraphrased the poem with Bill at the center...

"Sometimes things don't go right for me, Bill," I said. "And it seems that those you have tried to help the most don't seem to care. When this occurs I come home feeling discouraged and blue. Then something amazing happens. A little man suddenly appears. He is sort of dirty, has a runny nose, and sometimes he has not behaved as well as he should have during the day. And it seems like I start picking up his playthings from the time I step out of the car until I reach the front door.

"So there I stand—tired, discouraged, and hurt in the

heart. And suddenly that little man makes me feel better by saying just two powerful words: 'Hi Dad.' Bill, that little man with the wondrous power is you."

Bill felt the joy of giving that night and, I believe, has been immensely pleased with what he has given me ever since.

Our commitment to family influenced our choices of financial investments. With what little extra money we had, we started by purchasing real estate. We made this choice as opposed to other forms of investment so that Bill and his brothers could experience ownership. When they skated on our frozen lake in the winter, swam in it during the summer, and explored the property while playing, they would develop an appreciation for the land. They could feel, smell, and see it— a tangible holding they could relate to. How could a father explain municipal bonds, commodities, or stock certificates? How could young boys relate to paper transactions?

In 1966, my real estate partner, Van, approached me with an interesting proposition. He had heard of a large, potentially valuable piece of property soon to be placed on the market. Van drove me to the site located in a nearby city undergoing rapid growth.

I liked the location, price, and potential. As we drove back to my office, I asked, "Will we buy this land, hold onto it for a while, and then sell it for whatever profit we can realize, as we've done on our other investments?"

"No, Keith," Van answered. "We'd have to develop this piece ourselves—you know, build apartments and stores, deal with contractors and subcontractors, and that sort of thing. I'd need twenty hours a week of your time to do it. I'll put in sixty. And believe me, when we're through, I have no doubt that we'll each be a million or two richer."

Two million dollars—twenty hours a week. Two million dollars—twenty hours a week. Van's words echoed in my mind as I sat alone in my study later that evening.

What should I do? Fifty-five to sixty hours of my time each week—time that could not be spared or shared—was taken up by the duties of my judgeship. The twenty hours a week for property development would have to be borrowed from the time I spent with my family and teaching a Sunday school class.

I made my decision. I called Van the next day and told him I couldn't get involved in a real estate venture that would take time away from my wife and sons, no matter how much money I would make. Van, as it turned out, was greatly relieved; for he had agonized over the same considerations and arrived at the same decision.

The people who bought the land did make two million dollars. But there is no doubt in my mind that we made the right decision.

In 1969, after spending ten years as the judge of our city's municipal court, I resigned. I did this largely for Bill. When I was first elected, Bill was only four years old. I had promised myself that I would not be the judge of our city court when he entered high school. I thought that Bill, as a struggling insecure teenager, would be at an uncomfortable stage of life; being labeled the judge's son would be an additional pressure. When Bill was halfway through the eighth grade, I said goodbye to the court system, a decision I have never regretted.

Our sons' influences never ceased to amaze me. I strove to be an exemplary father, initially from a sense of duty, then out of love. I tried to consider what was best for the boys, not merely Audrey and me. This method of decision-making has succeeded thus far. I cannot think of a single time that a decision based on looking at the world through our sons' eyes was not the right way to go.

4 And the Word Became Flesh

Two, three, four runners came into view. Five, six, seven. Where is he? I wondered. For a moment I was struck by the sickening thought that perhaps Bill was forced to drop out. He had never quit a race, no matter how much pain he felt or how far he fell behind. There was always the first time—a severe charley horse or side stitch could happen to anyone.

Eight, nine, ten and still no sign of Bill. Thirty-three, thirty-six, thirty-nine. There he was, erect, his right shoulder lurching up and down with each pumping motion of his loose-swinging arms. His style was unmistakable.

My heart sank. Thirty-nine runners outpaced Bill. Even before I could see his facial features, I knew Bill was straining too hard. When he had won a league meet a few weeks before, he seemed at times to glide along the ground. Now he seemed to be pressing, pushing. Every muscle bulged. Even his veins were visible.

I wished he could stop and tell me, "I feel fine, Dad," or "My stomach is cramped," or "My legs feel heavy." Another runner hemmed him in on the inside. As Bill got a little closer, I could see his face racked with pain. My thoughts flashed on another face once filled with pain—the face of Christ.

Many of us have been influenced by a passage of Scripture. The words that have prevailed upon my mind, heart, and soul for many years appear in the first chapter of the Gospel of John. The writer's fingers must have trembled as he endeavored to express the overwhelming truth revealed to him, "And the Word became flesh and dwelt among us" (John 1:14).

How often I thought about those words. The more I thought about them, the more I envisioned a God who looked down from heaven and became increasingly frustrated by the fact that we did not comprehend His love for us.

He had given mankind His laws. He even numbered them one through ten, but we still didn't understand. Through His prophets He sent more words, but still men and women did not fathom the full meaning of His love. We did not understand, and we did not respond.

God must have realized that we would never learn of His redemptive love by communicating to us with words, laws, rules, and commandments. We simply do not understand them because we are not words, laws, rules, and commandments. He had to wrap up His message of love for us in the person of Jesus Christ.

When that personality bled, we understood because we bleed. When He was lonely, deserted, betrayed, denied, when He suffered and died, we understood because we can relate to these conditions as humans. God's redemptive process of love culminated in the person of Jesus Christ.

When I took the bench in the Municipal Court of Royal Oak, Michigan, most of the offenders who stood before me did not comprehend the meaning of our laws, statutes, and commandments. The offenders were flesh and blood, not words and laws. As a result, our decrees and punishments failed more often than not to rehabilitate. These wayward youths needed a demonstration of a better way to live, something they could relate to emotionally.

As the judge, all I could do was look at these defendants for a few seconds after they were found guilty and say, "You pay a fine," or "You go to jail," or both. Nothing else. We processed offenders like slaughterhouse cattle, their fate already sealed with doom. We fined them, one after another, and sent them to jail without hesitation. The relentless process continued all day long, day after day, month after month, year after year.

Here we saw all this human need, and all we did in the court was punish. The defendant might be a deserted or abused teenager. Our answer: fine and jail. He might be an alcoholic, sick and alone. Fine and jail. He might have had a quarrel with his wife and, out of anger, hit someone though he had never done so before. Fine and jail. He might be suffering from some manic disorder. Fine and jail. We were tough. We knew what to do. Punish. Punish. Punish.

And, God forgive us, we were ignorant. Many offenders returned again and again. We were supposed to solve these offenders' problems and make our streets safe. In many cases we created more problems. We made our streets perilous by increasing bitterness and aggression in troubled youths—young men already shackled by insurmountable problems. They had hurt society; society punished them in return. When released from prison they were so embittered towards society, they hurt us even more. And we responded with yet more punishment. The tragic pattern became all too clear. Of those who committed violent crimes—murder, rape, and armed robbery—approximately 80 percent had appeared before a lower court on lesser charges.

Think of it, 80 percent of our worst criminals began as young, minor offenders. We punished them instead of helping them. They learned well from us—their later acts of serious crime were often ruthless as they retaliated against a callous society.

We had to change the system and we did. We embodied our heartfelt concern for the offenders in the form of dedicated personalities from our community—volunteer citizens, whether Jew, Christian, atheist, man, woman, black, white, retiree, or young college student. These volunteers involved themselves one-on-one with our offenders, showing them a better way to live. And because help came in the form of human flesh and blood, the offender understood. The word of law became flesh in the inspiring volunteers.

This was the beginning of a rehabilitative process that has succeeded time and again. The volunteer program took fifteen to twenty hours of my time over and above the forty hours a week I worked as judge. My contribution paled in comparison with that of others. Hundreds of volunteers donated time totaling more than 50,000 hours a year. We analyzed each offender's unique problems and provided the right combination of discipline and treatment. Subsequent research proved that our rate of repeat crime was reduced by 75 percent compared with a similar court that did not use volunteers.*

Volunteers in Probation began in 1959. Fourteen years later 300,000 citizen volunteers were involved with offenders in some two thousand courts, jails, prisons, and juvenile institutions across the country. The word of law had truly become flesh and it continues today. As of 1987 there were 5,657,000

*For the complete story of this research and the once-unique, now-widespread rehabilitative program, see *First Offender* by Joe Alex Morris, published by Funk and Wagnalls, available from Hon. Keith Leenhouts, 830 Normandy, Royal Oak, MI 48073. Information about using volunteers in courts, prisons, jails, and juvenile institutions is also available upon request.

citizen volunteers active in 4000 institutions. An estimated 7,000,000 volunteers were active as of 1997.

Bill and I discussed the concept of the "word becoming flesh" on numerous occasions—in our sauna, on wilderness canoe trips, at bedtime, and in the high school Sunday school class I taught. We decided that this particular concept was difficult to explain or grasp due to the paradoxical nature of Christ.

For instance, we are instructed to be humble because Christ was humble. Yet, when He was called good, He protested that only God was good. But on another occasion, He stated, "I am the way, and the truth, and the life; no one comes to the Father, but by me"(John 14:6).

Humble? Majestic? Or both?

We should be gentle because Christ was gentle. "Gentle Jesus meek and mild. Tenderly watch over this little child," has been sung for generations. "Turn the other cheek," Christ Himself said. Yet He drove the moneychangers out of the temple with a fierceness and courage which has rarely been matched.

Gentle? Fierce? Or both?

And we should be forgiving because He was forgiving. On the cross He cried out, "Father, forgive them; for they know not what they do" (Luke 23:34). On another occasion He told His disciples to forgive seventy times seven, meaning, there is no limit. Yet He also said that he who harmed a child would be better off had he never been born. It would have been better for the offender if a millstone was tied around his neck and he was cast into the depths of the sea.

Forgiving? Unforgiving? Or both?

In our six-by-six Finnish sauna, bodies wet with perspiration, eyes smarting with sweat, and faces glowing red from the 180-degree heat, we pondered the mysteries of Christ's life. Only by study, thought, and prayer could these apparent contradictions and paradoxes be resolved. Only then could we begin to know Him, appreciate His complex nature, and embrace the full meaning of the word becoming flesh.

I remember the first trip I took with Bill into an expansive wilderness area in northern Minnesota and Canada. No roads scarred this virgin forestland. Airplanes, banned from flying over head, relinquished the sky to clouds, gulls, and soft singing breezes. In this lush and rugged setting, dotted with thousands of lakes, I explained to Bill the temptation Jesus experienced in the wilderness after His baptism.

The evening was star-filled. Bill listened attentively. As I talked I knew he heard not only me, but also the forlorn call of loons echoing across the water and the rhythmic lapping of small waves against our island.

Concluding, I asked Bill, "What would have happened had Jesus used His great power for His own purposes to gain wealth, power, or food?"

The flickering of the dying fire cast dancing shadows on our tent. Bill contemplated for a few moments before he answered, "If Jesus had used those powers for His own self, Dad, God would have taken all His powers away." What great insight from our young son. What a moment for me—to experience the depth of this four-year-old's understanding.

While camping a few years later, we placed a burning candle upon a large rock ledge at our shoreline site and left for an evening of surface casting for bass. It was dark when we returned. I could barely see Bill paddling in the front of the canoe. But, from over two miles away, we could see our candle, a beacon glowing in the dark. We said our prayers as we paddled toward that brightness, and I sang some hymns.

We gave and received, Bill and I, and, as a consequence, shared the gift of those memorable two miles that are forever uniquely ours. To the best of our ability, we lived love. We didn't have to talk about it, for the commandment, "love one another" became flesh. That's how we grasped the meaning of love.

I carried my love for Bill in my heart, body, mind, and soul so that the word "love" truly became flesh. If Bill could sense God's love and give God his love, then I had done my job as a father. If not, I had failed. To me it was that simple.

An early indication that I had succeeded came when Bill and I were driving to a Sunday school weekend retreat during his freshman year in high school. As we gazed upon the glorious star-filled night, I inquired, "Bill we don't talk about it very much but do you understand that in my life Christ is what it's all about?"

"Dad, it comes over loud and clear," he replied.

Rather than simply preaching words to them, I tried to instill godly behavior in our sons by the way I lived my life. I first knew I had at least partially succeeded during Bill's sophomore year. He had gained the seventh and last spot on the varsity cross-country team that fall.

In a minor race run just before the regionals, the entire team finished poorly. Bill ran the slowest he had run all year. Then, at the reserve meet, a boy we will call "Steve" finished with a faster time than Bill's.

For the first time that year the coach had to choose who would run in the regionals: Bill or Steve. Steve had run faster than Bill in the previous meet, but Bill had run more consistently throughout the year. Considering the importance of the regionals, we wondered what the coach's decision would be. If the coach chose Steve, I worried that Bill would be adversely affected, interpreting his coach's choice as another defeat. On Friday Bill told us the coach had decided to run Steve. Bill did not appear disappointed, and I wondered why. That night, in the sauna, Bill told me the entire story...

"The team voted for me to run in the regional meet. But after the meeting I went to the coach and said, 'Coach, I think Steve should run. You see, if he doesn't he might get discouraged and quit, and we need him on the team next year. Besides, I'll still be your friend whether I run or not. But if you don't let Steve run, he might not be friends with you anymore, and I think Steve needs your friendship.'"

I paused midway from wiping perspiration from my eyes and blinked a long stare at my son. "Bill," I whispered, "do you realize what a truly Christ-like act that was?"

He offered a simple shrugged reply, "Oh, I didn't think about that. I just did what I thought was best for Steve and for the team."

I was pleased. Our son was developing a spontaneous Christ-like life.

The next Saturday Steve's performance was off. After several more disappointing races, he quit the team. Bill won his race at the reserve meet, bettering Steve's best time.

Bill and I talked about victory and how to handle success that night after the reserve meet. Not that Bill had handled his first triumph badly. On the contrary, he shook hands with the other runners after the race and trotted off by himself to cool down—exactly as he had done throughout his defeats. For sixteen years we had discussed losses and how to handle them. Now, for a change, we enjoyed examining what to do after winning.

Judge Arthur E. Moore, a former juvenile judge of our county and my judicial ideal, was one of several men Bill and I admired. Judge Moore was my Sunday school teacher in high school. He initiated innovative programs as a jurist back in the thirties and forties, three decades ahead of his time.

One of his acts was establishing Camp Oakland. This facility enabled delinquent kids to enjoy a country setting, live in a comfortable farm-like home, and learn hands-on skills. They practiced discipline. Most of all, they learned to live with love. Remarkable things have happened on those acres during the intervening years.

When I first became a judge, Judge Moore told me, "Keith, if you do things differently, get ready to have mud thrown in your face." He spoke with sincerity and sadness. He knew. He loved kids and had instituted many judicial reforms to help them. Few judges had his vision and foresight. Some responded by throwing mud his way.

What an awakening I was in for once the newness wore off my robes. I found it incredible that the most our system could offer was Fine and Punish. Fine and Punish. The process had to be changed, and there was only one way to do it —volunteer power fueled by the people of our city.

In October 1965, *Reader's Digest* printed the first story about Royal Oak. The article, *"Royal Oak Aids Its Problem Youth,"* was to have a profound effect on the spread of the idea to other courts. The article, however, also caused unrest among members of the judicial system.

Some judges were openly critical of the concept of lay volunteers becoming involved with criminals in an effort to assist the defective judicial system. They scoffed at such a preposterous proposal. As the idea grew into a popular reality, I sometimes became the target for their opposition and mudslinging.

"Bill," I told my son after the reserve meet, "as you win and become better and better, your head will rise farther and farther above the crowd. Remember, someone will seize the opportunity to bring you down to their size. Mud really hurts when it hits you in the face."

5 Lessons from Buster

Thirty-nine runners outpaced Bill on the flat. He did not have a kick—a final burst of speed—that he could rely on at the end of the race. He knew, and so did I, that he could not afford to fall far behind.

Then...a change in pattern. Bill moved to the outside and began to pass other runners. Gaining momentum as he passed, he raised a clenched right fist to signify he was okay. His face glowed with confidence. He was making his move.

"Go Blue!" I yelled to encourage all our team's runners. But deep in my heart I knew who Blue was—"Billy Blue." Bill had picked up this nickname from a teammate when he first made varsity as a sophomore.

As he swept by, he continued to advance through the runners. If the determined look on his face mirrored his thoughts, he was thinking, *Man, there's no way I'm going to louse this up. I'm going to run the best race of my life.*

Could his desire and our love carry him over the remaining miles to the victory he dreamed of? Now, at last, the possibility brightened. "Go Blue!" I hollered as he disappeared over the next hill.

*B*oyd Rucket...*It's strange to be thinking of him now...*

Rugged and weathered, Boyd was a farmer who worked the rolling, golden wheat fields of southeastern Washington. During the summer of 1950, I was on break between my first two years of law school. I drove truck for Boyd, hauling wheat from his fields to a granary in nearby Pomeroy.

On a hot, dry afternoon, I was about to drive to the granary. Boyd ran over to the truck, his rough voice huffing, "Keith, there're some cows in the field just south of our barn. After you drop this load off, take Buster and get him to drive the cows back where they belong."

Buster was Boyd's dog, a handsome butterscotch and white collie-German shepherd. Since starting to work for Boyd, Buster had been my constant companion, keeping me company on the treks from field to granary and back again.

By the time I said, "Okay," Buster had leaped through the truck's open window to take his customary position at my side. We were great friends, and I almost thought of him as my dog.

After unloading the grain in town, Buster and I hurried back to Boyd's farmhouse. There we exchanged the rusting, old wooden-boxed truck for a new jeep and headed across the roadless field to the grazing cows. I vaulted out of the topless jeep and, with Buster playfully nipping at my heels and shirt sleeves, jogged to the south of the cows.

"Buster," I commanded, "drive them back where they belong."

Circling north, Buster ignored my shouts and began driving the cows south, away from Boyd's barn. I tried waving them off, but Buster's skillful herding outweighed my efforts.

He returned, obviously pleased with himself, and tried

to nuzzle his nose under my clenched fist, expecting praise from me for a job well done. His wagging tail dropped as I jerked my hand away and grumbled, "What do you think you're doing?"

Now, farther out in the field, I led Buster by his collar southward, past the cows, and told him, "This time do it right. Put the cows where they belong." Rather than circling the herd, Buster carefully picked his way through them until he was once again on their north side. Again he drove them south.

Sweat poured down my face. Flushed from heat and frustration, I wanted to give up but couldn't let Boyd down without one more attempt. Buster had his own ideas. Ignoring all my pleas, screams, and threats, he drove the bellowing herd over a hill, through a creek, up a brushy embankment to a weathered, sway-backed barn belonging to "Old Bill," a bachelor farmer and Boyd's nearest neighbor.

"One of us is stupid!" I gasped with all the voice I could muster after scrambling through brush and reaching Old Bill's barn. And that's only a little bit of what I said. But Buster wasn't angry; he merely looked up at me with hurt in those big brown eyes. We were such good friends, and he couldn't understand my anger.

We sped back to Boyd's house, where I quickly exited the jeep and scrambled back into the truck. I slammed the door, started the motor, and began to pull away from the stupid animal that had caused me so much trouble. Buster looked so sad and forlorn that I relented, saying, as I opened the door, "Okay, come on, Buster. After all, you're only a dumb dog. I shouldn't expect more from you, I guess."

When we got back to the wheat fields, the buzzing anger in my head suddenly sank like a lead weight to the pit of my stomach. There sat Boyd's combine—idle—with a full load of wheat. Not only had I failed to drive the cows back to Boyd's barn, but I had committed the wheat truck driver's cardinal sin. I had failed to load on the run and allowed the combine to stop, an action not allowed except for lunch breaks and repairs.

I pulled the truck to a halt. Boyd ran over, angry and shouting, "Where in the world have you been, Keith?" Chagrined, I reported the whole story of how, despite all my efforts, Buster had driven the cows to Old Bill's barn.

All the wind-, sun-, and time-etched cracks on Boyd's square brown face turned upward into a great smile, followed by a laugh that turned into a howl. He gasped, "What's wrong with that, Keith? Those are Old Bill's cows."

I stared down at my dusty boots for a few seconds without saying a word. My glance shifted to Buster and my eyes glistened as I realized what I had done. Jumping up and placing his large paws on my chest, Buster licked my face in acceptance of my humble apology.

"Buster, one of us is stupid." Those words still echo in my mind. They were true all right; one of us was stupid, but it wasn't Buster. That was a humbling experience I have never forgotten.

Nine years later as an elected judge, I discovered that sitting on the bench is anything but a humbling process. Like the Roman centurion of old, I would say "Come," and they would come, "Go," and they would go. I needed a reminder. I slipped a quote from the book of Micah (Micah 6:8) under the glass that covered my desktop—with one slight addition: "And what does the Lord require of you but to do justice, and to love kindness, and to walk humbly with your God? ...and...*Remember Buster.*"

My experience with Buster helped me meet the difficult task of retaining some sense of humility while being what a judge is: a small god in his courtroom.

Each day as I entered the courtroom, I uttered a silent prayer for understanding, patience, and courage to make the right decisions, be they punishment, rehabilitation, or a combination of both. And I always ended the prayer with my version of a courtroom amen: "Remember Buster."

6 Inspirations from the Courtroom

The championship cross-country course wound through rolling hills and green velvet valleys. Normally dotted with picnicking families or young lovers, the hills became transformed into a battlefield of relentless striving for the *thinclads*. Every rise in elevation, no matter how slight, depleted their energy and challenged their stamina as they battled each other and fatigue to finish the race.

As I watched I wondered what force drove these weary runners. Surely, some ran for status, prestige, glory, and fame. Did Bill? Or was he motivated by inspirational thoughts? Although we had talked about the obligations that accompany victory, its frequent accomplices—fame and wealth—had not been discussed.

"**D**ad, who is the most successful man you know?" Bill had asked as we entered our sauna a few months before the big race.

"I can't answer that," I said, "until we define success."
I paused, letting the steam billow around us while Bill stretched and got comfortable.

" I think a friend of mine once summed it up when he said, 'True success is the ability to accept and give love.' If this is the definition of success—and I believe it is—then my pick would be Ralph Shepard."

" The retired school superintendent?"

"Yep. The one and only. I miss him even now," I answered, settling into our steamy world as I prepared to explain why I will always hold Ralph in such high regard.

I had first met Ralph some ten years before. He was retired and had dropped by my office to ask if he could assist with our volunteer program. The sight of Ralph prompted me to recall what Will Rogers once said. "Anyone over forty is responsible for how he looks." Well, I looked at this gray-haired, smiling man standing before me and instantly saw the very personification of love. His whole face, his whole being seemed to express love.

After we talked about the program, I said, "Ralph, we are going to call you a presentence investigator. But please don't let that confuse you. We just want you to love people."

From that moment until the day he died some years later, Ralph loved the defendants who appeared before our court. What Ralph did for them was invaluable. In a typical case a teenage defendant would plead or be found guilty. I would declare, "Guilt having been determined, the court will refer you to the presentence department for an investigation. Sentencing will be adjourned for three weeks until we receive their report and study it."

The defendant—hatred, fear, frustration, and anger welling up inside—would resist the urge to hit me only because he knew he would get into worse trouble. Then he would stalk out of the courtroom. Day after day I stared into hate-filled eyes. But when the defendant entered Ralph's office, Ralph did not, or perhaps could not, see hatred. He only saw hurt in those eyes.

"During the first twenty minutes of our presentence investigation, the defendant screams, shouts, swears, and snarls at me," Ralph told me. "But I like to smoke a pipe during these interviews. Now that I'm old I have to fumble for the pouch and can never find it very fast. When I do find it, it takes me a long time to pack it right. I never get it right the first time, so I have to unload and repack. I usually have to repeat this whole operation two or three times before I am satisfied. Obviously, during this time, I can't yell back and defend the court or myself. Packing my pipe requires too much concentration. I can only listen.

"Finally, after twenty minutes I take my first triumphant puff on the pipe, lean back, and say, 'Son, let's chat.'"

How can you stay mad at a person whom you have screamed at for twenty minutes, when all he says in reply is, "Son, let's chat"?—especially when you realize he is sincerely interested in you and wants to know where and how it hurts.

And chat they did. No professional could have afforded the time. Most presentence interviews, in the few lower courts that conduct them at all, take fifteen minutes or less in typical misdemeanor cases. But in many cases Ralph met the defendant shortly after 8 a.m. At noon they headed to the restaurant across the street for a sandwich. Sometimes they even returned to Ralph's office after lunch for additional dialogue.

This happened time after time. Many defendants—so angry, so hostile when they walked out of the courtroom— would, after talking with Ralph, return and take a seat in the back of the room. They would sit patiently, sometimes for two hours, waiting for a recess. Then they would seek me out and say, "Judge, I have a question. Can Mr. Shepard be my probation officer?"

Ralph did what no one ever did for them before. He enhanced the defendant's dignity by listening. Ralph knew the secret: If you really want to make someone feel important, worthwhile, and good, listen to him. As Ralph himself said, "Enemies talk, friends listen." To me he personified the title of a book by John W. Drakeford, *The Awesome Power of the Listening Ear.*

"Keith, the trouble with judges is they only listen to words," Ralph once chided me. "Don't listen to the words. They only confuse. When people talk, listen to their music."

How Ralph listened to music. When a defendant snarled, "I hate you old man," Ralph heard, "I'm all alone. Please help me."

At the end of a four-hour presentence investigation, Ralph would ask the young man or woman to bring in their mother or dad or someone else to speak on their behalf. This request would have been soundly rejected at the start of a conversation; but as the defendant came to regard Ralph as a friend, he nearly always complied.

When Ralph met with the adult, he verbally disarmed that person. His first question was, "Tell me the good things about your son." His genuine concern proved irresistible.

Ralph sought the good things about defendants. He told me, "You have plenty people and their reports to relate the bad things—the police record, the arresting officer, the complaining witness. I'll be the one to give you good news. Don't ignore it. The bad must be dealt with. But the good is needed to build upon."

Ralph's reports might read, "This boy lives next door to an elderly widow. For years he has been mowing her lawn and won't accept any payment." Or, "This girl lives across the street from a young divorcee with three children. She baby-sits while the mother goes to school one night a week. She won't take any money for her time. She says, 'I have to study anyway. I might as well study on one side of the street as the other.'"

A few days later in the courtroom, Ralph's eyes would twinkle with delight and love. "Mr. Shepard tells us you have been mowing the lawn of that widow for many years," I would say. "He tells us a lot of other things about you. We think you are a fine young man who should never have been involved in this kind of conduct. We also think you are not going to get into any more trouble. We expect you to accomplish some worthy things with your life and look forward to our year of probation together. We anticipate dismissing this case in a year—after you have proven to our probation department that Mr. Shepard is right."

Ralph liked that. He always said, "You know, Judge, people nearly always give you what you expect. Expect hate and you will get it. Expect failure and you will get it. Moreover, if you expect accomplishment and achievement, you will usually get it."

Ralph Shepard possessed the key ingredient needed to be effective. He was a decent human being.

I fear that in our quest for brilliance we can lose the importance of being human. I have become concerned by the emphasis of graduate schools, especially law schools, on being smart. The dean of a large and prestigious law school told me, "We are very proud of our law school. Over 50 percent of our seniors could not get in if they were applying as freshmen this year."

I should have held my tongue. Instead, I said, "Oh, that's a shame. Almost without exception, the top students I have known have done very little for other people. Many have gone on to make a lot of money for themselves. But of course, there is little value in that. Nearly all the students I know of who have gone on to effectively serve their fellowmen have been the B and C students." The dean became angry.

Ralph was an artisan in his manner of addressing the emotional turmoil and hidden character of youthful offenders. In his enthusiasm, however, Ralph often overlooked factual information such as home address, and family and school background. Of course we needed these facts. For gathering this information, we utilized the services of volunteer Lou Loeffert, a retiree who had investigated labor disputes for forty-eight years.

Lou proved to be an uncanny investigator. He could learn more about you in fifteen minutes than most people could find out in years. He would gather the facts—the work record, the school record, the criminal record, the family records, and all the other information important to a good investigation. His thoroughness and the crispness of his mind were a never-ending source of amazement.

The third member of our team was Bill H., a retiree and recovered alcoholic. After many years of drinking and dealing with the troubles alcohol brings, Bill underwent hospitalization and sought professional help. He then joined Alcoholics Anonymous. Bill met with each defendant who appeared before us on a drinking-related offense. He determined whether the offender was an alcoholic, experimenter, or an occasional drinker who got a little carried away.

Volunteer psychiatrists, psychologists, medical doctors, attorneys, and other professionals supplemented our three-man team of investigators. They contributed four vital elements to our investigation: helped the judge determine the proper sentence; diverted misplaced medical cases from the criminal justice system; developed a probational plan of rehabilitation; and encouraged us to expand until we possessed every rehabilitative technique available.

Ralph Shepard added a fifth vital element. He prepared the offender for a probation experience based on tough love. Because of Ralph, Lou, Bill, and the others, I believe we had the finest presentence department in the country.

I blinked sweat from my eyes. As if reading my mind, Bill said, "You're missing him right now, aren't you, Dad?" I looked at his slim body, relaxed and prone on the bench, one arm thrown up over his eyes, and realized, *How well he sees inside me without even looking.*

"Ralph transformed the entire atmosphere of our courtroom and probation department, Son. And he worked that miracle with his genuine love and concern."

I shared with Bill one other time I had experienced the phenomenon of a changed atmosphere. I was far from home in unfamiliar territory. I entered a courthouse and a voice rang out, "Can I help you, sir?" This took me by surprise, as I had never before been greeted that way in a probation department. Glancing around I saw a young man in a wheelchair sitting under a sign that read, *Information.*

He regarded my quizzical expression with a warm smile and continued, "It sure is a nice day, isn't it? Are you a stranger in our city?"

I nodded and he asked, "Who do you want to see?" When I replied, he gave me directions and I turned to leave. A cheerful, "Have a good day," lingered behind me.

This pleasant departure from the usual cold, impersonal atmosphere of probation departments left me with a sense of wonder. A few minutes later I was in the office of the chief probation officer on my mission of helping them start a volunteer program. When I mentioned the wheel-chaired youth downstairs, the officer told me the youth had been a high school athlete, but before graduation an automobile accident had left him permanently paralyzed. Then the officer made an odd request. "Do me a favor," he said. "As you talk to people today, ask them who the most important employee is in this building.

I would appreciate it."

I talked to about fifteen members of the probation department that day. At the end of each conversation I asked, "Who is the most important employee in this building?" Everyone said, without hesitation, "That's easy. The boy in the wheelchair. Before he came here, nearly every parent came in angry and ready to fight. I used to hate coming to work. But now a completely different atmosphere exists. Working is fun. When parents and others come in mad and upset, the young man greets them with a smile on his face and in his voice. They talk for a few minutes. As they leave he says something like, 'I'm glad that you have probation officer Brown. You'll like him. He loves kids. Not only does he work here fifty hours a week, but he spends another ten hours coaching Little League teams.'"

The wheel-chaired youth reminded me of Ralph Shepard. His genuine love was infectious.

It was time for Bill and me to leave our redwood retreat. As we gathered our towels, Bill said, "It's like you said in the beginning...right? About being able to give and accept love. Ralph Shepard could do that...right?"

"Yes," I replied, "And he taught me what success is all about. From that perspective I consider him the most successful man I have known." I hoped Bill understood what I had tried pass on—that success could be defined in terms other than wealth and prestige. Yes, I hoped I had been able to communicate this to Bill. What greater truth could a father teach his son?

A wise bit of advice came from our friend Ralph, though Kipling said it first: "Be slow to judge. We know little of what has been done and nothing about what has been resisted." I kept this saying under the glass desktop in my courtroom right next to "Remember Buster."

Be slow to judge. We know little of what has been done and nothing about what has been resisted. It's not difficult to decide guilt or innocence in most cases. Sentencing a man—deciding how he will spend his immediate future and how he will spend the rest of his life—that is the challenge.

I had been serving on the bench for only a few weeks when two young men, aged seventeen and nineteen, appeared before me. I listened to their plea of not guilty, and a jury trial was slated. Testimony revealed that the younger brother, George, was driving down a street and saw a police officer. Apparently trying to impress his passenger, George screamed at the officer, calling him the most obscene names imaginable. Then he screeched his tires and sped away. The policeman jumped into his squad car in rapid pursuit. George didn't realize that his brother, Mark, also joined the chase.

Quickly overtaking George's car and forcing it into a parking lot, the officer attempted to pull George out of the door. He resisted and they struggled. George's brother caught up and yelled, "I'm his brother, I'm his brother. Be careful! He has a heart condition."

The policeman either didn't hear or ignored Mark and continued pulling George, who struggled in vain. Mark shouted his warning a second time but still to no avail. Mark then stepped between the two and shoved them apart.

At that moment more police arrived, summonded by their radios. George and Mark were arrested. George was charged with disorderly conduct and Mark with interfering with an officer in the performance of his duties.

The jury listened to the evidence and returned to the courtroom after deliberating for two hours. It seemed obvious to me that George was guilty. And such was the jury's verdict—guilty as charged. But what about Mark? I hoped the jury would find him not guilty. Although we have feelings and opinions, judges are not allowed to convey them to the jury. "In the second case," the foreman intoned, "we also find the defendant guilty." I felt a sinking sensation in my stomach and a heavy burden on my heart. I adjourned both cases for final determination and sentencing. I had to make a decision. I could render judgement in accordance with the guilty verdict of the jury, or I could rescind their decision and find Mark not guilty.

While spending the long Labor Day weekend at picturesque Lake Vermillion in northern Minnesota, I pondered the two brothers. The walleyes were biting, the sun was shining, and I was eight hundred miles from home. Yet I couldn't take my mind off those cases. So much seemed to be at stake.

George was clearly guilty—no doubt about that. It was just a matter of sentencing. Since this was his first offense as an adult, and since we didn't have a volunteer program yet, a fine would be appropriate.

But Mark? In my heart I knew the jury's decision was wrong and the case against Mark should be dismissed. The consequences of such a decision were immense. The arresting officer had often been heard accusing the court of going soft on criminals. If I overruled the jury and set Mark free, the policeman would be outraged. He would complain to his peers how there was no sense in even taking a case to court. And he would have listening ears.

As for me, nearly everyone evaluates a judge by what he does in his first few months on the bench. In the blink of an eye, a new jurist may be labeled as "a tough law enforcement judge" or "a soft defendant's judge." First labels stick.

I talked to the veteran clerk to ascertain whether any of my predecessors had ever set aside a jury's verdict. She did not know a judge could do such a thing and in her ten years as clerk had never seen it done.

What was the greater good—maintain the image of the court in the eyes of the police so they would continue to bring in the appropriate cases? Or do what I felt was right: dismiss this case knowing full well that some policemen would consider this unjust and shirk their duty. I could, of course, do only one thing.

With my decision made, I returned to the bench after our weekend in Minnesota. I announced to the defendants, the police, and everyone else in court, "The defendant George Smith is found guilty and is sentenced to pay a fine of $50. In the second case the defendant Mark Smith is found not guilty."

Turmoil ensued. The mother of the defendants was furious, believing both her boys not guilty. The brothers stalked out of the courtroom and returned to their home angry with the stupid judge who had found George guilty and made him pay a fine. The policeman stomped from the courtroom and did not bring another case to court for a long time. During that extended period I wondered how many offenders were ignored or let go by the brothers' arresting officer and others he influenced.

Friends who had supported me when I ran for judge asked me why I let a kid go after the jury had found him guilty. Fortunately, they came to me so I could explain what had happened. I'm sure hundreds of others who heard the same story just labeled me soft on crime without bothering to seek the truth.

I have known for most of my life that wrong choices are often the easiet and most convenient. At least it appears that way. No doubt, sentencing Mark would have pleased the most people. But a decision based on pleasing people ignores the right choices that must be made. God gives us discernment to differentiate right from wrong. Predictable responses to our decision, whether favorable or disagreeable, should not sway us from making proper choices.

Regrettably, I did not always do the right thing. I shared some of these painful memories with my sons. My worst experience was a case in which two human lives were lost.

Tough at eighteen, "Jack" was called "The Enforcer" by his gang. He took it upon himself to avenge the wrongs suffered by any of his buddies. For no apparent reason one day, Jack walked into a drive-in restaurant and attacked the guard, who was sitting in a booth. After hitting him repeatedly, Jack fled the scene, leaving the guard injured and dazed.

Arrested and brought before me, Jack pleaded not guilty. The jury, however, returned a guilty verdict. A twenty-four hour presentence investigation was conducted after the trial. The facts about his role as the hatchet man of his gang surfaced, along with a history of a dismal childhood.

It was a difficult case to sentence. Gang activity was just beginning in our city, and we wanted to squelch it. But Jack's personal needs also deserved consideration.

Jack was fined and ordered to make restitution for damages. In this case it meant paying the guard's doctor and hospital bills plus damages to the restaurant. We also sentenced him to thirty days in jail. At my request he was kept in an individual cell at the city lockup, rather than being thrown into a bullpen with other prisoners at the county jail.

Presentence files included reports from a volunteer psychiatrist and our own official staff. After reviewing the files it was clear to me we must do two things: first, convince the defendant that there is a right and wrong and that wrongdoing means punishment. Once that was dealt with by putting him in jail, there was a second need: help the defendant see that there was a better way to live. To accomplish this Jack would be assigned to group therapy sessions after he served his jail term. He would meet regularly with one of our volunteer psychiatrists and eight to twelve other probationers from our court.

Jail time in the isolated cell was difficult for Jack. On many occasions we had men request thirty days in the county jail rather than six days of individual lockup. Eventually, we came to equate one day in the city jail to five in the county.

After Jack had been incarcerated for seven days, two policemen that I respected requested that Jack be allowed to leave his cell during the day to wash police cars. I didn't believe he deserved this privilege, so I refused. Three days later they returned and repeated the request. I told them that if they still felt that way after three more days, I would consent. They came again three days later, and I granted their request as promised.

On two or three occasions after that, they and other officers requested a shortening of Jack's jail term. I refused until two days before his scheduled release. He was brought before me, and I carefully explained his terms of probation. Being a heavy drinker, he was required to attend the Alcohol and Drug Addiction School run by an excellent teacher, a recovered alcoholic. After three months of group psychotherapy, he would be assigned a one-on-one volunteer. He was well-programmed with meetings, reporting to someone four hours a week during the first two months, in addition to his weekly meeting with the regular staff.

One of the rules governing our group psychotherapy sessions required the psychiatrist to report only two facts about the group's attendees: whether the defendant showed up for the meetings and whether he had made any progress. This and nothing more.

When I talked to the psychiatrist after their fourth meeting, he told me Jack was attending and making progress. Off-the-record he added a rare third statement. "If Jack does not get himself into a hostile situation in the next two months or so, he will make it. He is really progressing." It appeared as though our procedure of being tough for the first month was working.

A few days later Jack was at a drive-in restaurant when another boy began taunting him. The teasing went beyond Jack's point of tolerance. He dashed out and returned with a gun. He shot and killed the boy.

Jack reappeared in our court, this time on the charge of murder. Because there was probable cause for believing Jack committed the crime, the case was sent to a higher court for trial. Jack was convicted of murder and sent to prison. About a year later we received word that he had been killed in a prison fight.

I have relived that case a thousand times. Why didn't I send a volunteer into the jail every day for those thirty days? We often assigned volunteers immediately, rather than after the jail term. Why not in this case? Why didn't we allow Jack to come out once a week for group meetings during those thirty days? Was it really necessary to be so tough for so long? Why didn't I heed the officers' requests sooner? A thousand "whys" have buffeted my soul. Jack's case will always serve as the ultimate example of failure for me as a judge. Not just one life, but two lives were lost. How much worse can you err?

We did what we honestly thought was best, but it did not work out that way. It is easy, of course, to tell the other guy not to second-guess and look back, but not yourself. It is easy to excuse others, but not yourself, particularly when your mistake involves the loss of human life.

Perhaps the most reassuring thing to tell yourself at such a time is that you are responsible for obedience, not results. If I did not believe this to be true, the burden of unfavorable cases would be unbearable. Obedience to God and self requires that we handle each case with meticulous care and do the best we possibly can. If we were held responsible for results, we would soon be driven to suicide.

7 The Fatherless

I alternately ran and walked with the other spectators to the three-quarter-mile mark where we would next see the runners flash by. There a century-old forest interrupted the roll of surrounding green hills. Runners entered this dark, damp maze along a narrow path—the forest's only breach—to emerge into daylight on the far side.

Weeks before while Bill had jogged around the course, Audrey, his brothers, and I had searched for the best vantage point to watch the runners as they approached the forest. Now, out of breath, I leaned against the scarred trunk of a familiar, aging pine. From here I could watch Bill for two hundred yards.

A lone runner burst over the crest of the hill—not Bill. Seconds seemed to tick off slowly as the solitary leader loped down the grassy slope and headed toward the sunless depths of the forest. Then a swarm of bodies, a moving entanglement of arms and legs appeared and spilled over the top of the hill. Two, three, four, five. *Where is our son?* Thoughts raced again—*Has he suffered a stomach cramp or a pulled muscle?*

As his father I was concerned.

Who is to be pitied more than the fatherless? How often in the Scriptures we see the fatherless singled out as *the least of these,* those to whom we owe the greatest duty. Time and again the point is made with force and clarity: the greatest duty is owed to the very least—the unfortunates, the down-trodden, the oppressed; those who continually suffer—those whom the Bible often characterizes by one word: *fatherless.*

"Defend the fatherless," demands Isaiah 1:17. "He executes justice for the fatherless," reads Deuteronomy 10:18.

Now and again I have wondered if our country should be the most pitied of all nations. So many fatherless victims and offenders passed through my courtroom that, at times, I regarded ours as an entire nation of fatherless people.

In one of my earliest cases, a twenty-eight-year-old father appeared charged with beating his wife. In order for a complaint and warrant to be issued, the court required his wife to appear beforehand. She described the events under oath in my office. In an exhausted and broken voice, she ended the interview with, "When he is sober he is wonderful. But when he drinks..."

A few hours later at the arraignment, the defendant pleaded guilty and asked to be sentenced immediately. "I'm guilty," he said and demanded, "Just go ahead and sentence me."

I told him I needed more information and asked the wife to testify under oath again. The defendant was mortified. As his wife began her testimony, I realized why he wanted to leave the courtroom as quickly as possible.

"Last night," his wife began, tears welling in her eyes and voice shaking, "he came home drunk. When I heard him slam the door I knew he was drunk. He always slams the door when he's drunk. Then I heard him downstairs, walking around, bumping against the walls. I was scared because he beats me when he comes home drunk like that.

"But this time was different. If it had only been me he beat and humiliated, I wouldn't have come to court. He stumbled up the stairs and began waking up our four children. The oldest is eight and the youngest is three. He screamed and swore at them and told them to get downstairs to the living room.

"I could hear the kids crying and screaming as they went downstairs. Then he came in to get me. 'You rotten—' he swore. 'You think that I don't know what's going on around here. You think I'm so stupid I don't know. But I do.' He grabbed me and pulled me out of bed, ripping my nightgown until I was almost naked. He grabbed me by the hair and arm and began to push, shove, and pull me down the stairs. By the time we got into the living room, I couldn't think or see straight, but I got a glimpse of the kids huddled in a back corner.

"Then he screamed at the kids, 'Now watch this you little brats. I'm going to show you who is boss. Make no mistake about it and don't forget this.' He started hitting me with his fist. He hit me in the eye, this one here that's all purple and swollen shut. I fell down but he yanked me off the floor and hit me in the stomach. I fell again and he pulled me up and hit me again. I don't know how many times he pulled me up off the floor and hit me before he stopped. Then he told the kids they'd better never forget who was the boss of his house and he staggered off to bed.

"The kids—just little children—and I waited until eight o'clock before we went to the police station. I wouldn't have gone to the police if it had only been me. I never have gone to the police before when he beat me. But this time it didn't involve just me. Why did he have to wake up the children and make them watch?"

As she ended her testimony, I looked away from her

battered face and let my eyes rest upon the defendant. He was crying. His children, sitting in the front row, were crying, too.

America, with all her wealth, power, and prestige, produced this young fatherless family—people to be pitied more than any others on earth.

"Mike" and I first met in 1962. He looked like many other seventeen-year-olds except for a distorted left eye. It rolled to one side, creating a grotesque appearance over which Mike had no control. As a result, he resembled the classic portrait of a thief who could not look you straight in the eye. Mike could not alter his appearance, so he lived up to the image, incurring a long record of shoplifting offenses both as a juvenile and as an adult.

When Mike appeared before our court charged with theft, we placed him on probation and assigned him to a volunteer. Months passed before the volunteer was able to build a good relationship with Mike. When he finally did, Mike told him, "People don't trust me. I look like a crook with my bad eye. I don't seem to be able to hold onto a job. When I can't find work, I don't have any money. But I still want things. The only way I can get them is to steal."

The volunteer referred Mike to one of several optometrists who volunteered their expertise to our program. He checked out Mike's wandering eye and discovered it was useless. Mike was blind in that eye.

The optometrist had a friend who was an eye surgeon. He told the surgeon about our volunteer program and about Mike. The surgeon agreed to remove the eye and donate a false eye that would eliminate Mike's distorted appearance.

Mike and his mother readily agreed. They were happy with the idea. But a few days later his mother told us Mike's

76

father disapproved of the operation. When she and Mike had gone home to tell the father the good news, he was drunk. When they asked him what he thought about the surgery, the father became angry and shouted, "No doctor is going to touch his eye. He was born that way, and that's the way he is going to stay. And besides, no doctor ever does anything for free. He'll send us a bill and sue us. No, Mike's not going to any doctor as long as I'm around!"

Again, it was a case of someone being fatherless even though he had a father. The story had a happy ending only because Mike's father left home and disappeared a few months later. Mike had the operation. His appearance was normalized, and he became a law-abiding citizen.

The Scriptures reveal more about the fatherless. God is described as, "Father of the fatherless," in Psalm 68:5. In Psalm 146:9 we read, "The Lord...upholds the fatherless."

"Harry" is another example. His case, which came to court in 1965, reminded me of two inner-city kids who were heard talking about a third boy they knew. One said to the other, "He's the luckiest guy in the world. He was born with a silver spoon in his mouth. He has a dad."

Harry had been sharing an apartment with four other seventeen-year-olds. All had dropped out of school and left home. Reading over the names, I immediately recognized Harry's—the same as one of Detroit's most distinguished attorneys. The youth's name bore a *junior*.

We decided to do a presentence investigation. In due course we discovered Harry was indeed the son of the attorney, whom I knew mostly by reputation. The father was the recognized authority in his field in Michigan, probably earning six figures annually.

We notified the parents and requested they come in,

as was our custom. Harry's mother responded and we talked with her. Her story was all too familiar. She said her husband had absolutely nothing to do with Harry ever since it became apparent in the fourth grade that Harry was not going to be an outstanding student—a *super-noodle*, as his father put it. Subsequently, all the father's attention turned to Harry's older brother and younger sister, who were *super-noodles*.

The father bragged to his friends about the other children in Harry's presence, but he never bragged about Harry. Harry began to withdraw and seemed to have less and less involvement with other people.

Then he found youngsters he could talk to, who would listen to him. All were outcasts even though they came from one of Detroit's most fashionable suburbs. When Harry began to get into trouble with the juvenile court, his father refused to see him except when ordered by the court.

We asked if Harry's father would meet with our staff. The mother doubted it very much, but we decided to try. Predictably, Harry's father did not respond.

I decided to call him. I identified myself on the phone and asked if he had received our request to participate in a presentencing conference. His answer was, "I'll tell you how to sentence him. Give him all the jail time you can—the full ninety days. And when he comes out and gets into more trouble, give him ninety days again. Then, when he commits a felony, put him in prison for the rest of his life."

Inside I wept for Harry. I could not feel more sorry for anyone than I did for this embittered teenager, orphaned by a living father who inflicted tremendous hurt. Again and again, I thanked God for my father who loved me, cared for me, and gave me one of the greatest gifts anyone can have—a real father.

The fatherless. More than the persecuted, more than the poor, more than the ill, more than anyone they are to be pitied. Repeatedly, the Scriptures tell us that our greatest duty is to the least of the least. And the very least are the fatherless.

At seventeen "Matt" appeared in court charged with being drunk and disorderly. His face was distorted by malformed teeth. Having a small mouth, his crowded teeth protruded at odd angles. We suspected they were also decayed because he had bad breath.

We assigned him to a volunteer. Several months later, after establishing a good relationship, the volunteer suggested Matt go to a dentist. Matt seemed at least mildly interested but added, "My mother has often wanted to take me, but my dad says he will beat us if she wastes his money like that. Sometimes my mother says, 'Let's go anyway, one more beating won't make that much difference.' But we have never been to a dentist."

The volunteer social worker arranged for Matt to go to the dental school at a nearby university. Under the direction of the professor, students in dental school fixed the teeth of the poor. Several visits later Matt's teeth were clean and repaired, and his appearance became normal.

"Now I feel like I can be somebody," Matt said. But the volunteer knew it took more than good teeth, and he suggested that Matt finish high school. At first Matt did not want to return to school. Gradually, he became interested and made the decision to start evening classes. The volunteer was elated.

At their next meeting, Matt opened the conversation by saying, "I told my dad I wanted to go to night school. He just looked at me, laughed, and said, 'You're too dumb to go to school. You should work a second job. Now, that would pay off. School will never pay off for a stupe like you.'"

The volunteer strained to hear Matt's final words,

words that seemed directed inward, "I guess Dad's right—I'm too stupid."

Not all cases coming to court involve the fatherless. Let no one get the idea that every time a young person gets into trouble with the law it can be traced to poor parenting. "Never and always" do not exist within the spectrum of human behavior. We are too complex for such absolutes.

Before becoming a judge I met a twelve-year-old boy called "Tom." I watched Tom develop through his teenage years. At seventeen he appeared before our court on a minor charge. During our presentence investigation a volunteer psychologist spent several hours with Tom and his parents. He reported, "Tom has caring parents. All of his brothers and sisters have done well. When Tom was young his parents sensed something was wrong with him and began to spend extra time with him. Nothing seemed to help. Tom's dad tried to get him interested in church league sports. He even coached Tom's team, but no improvement was observed. They also took him to psychologists and psychiatrists at an early age, but to no avail.

"I think the parents have done all they could with love, affection, and intelligence. I find no fault with them. Neither does Tom. But he keeps getting into more and more trouble. I'm afraid he is headed toward a felony. You know, Judge," the psychologist summed up for me, "there are three things that cause this kind of behavior. One is heredity, one is environment, and the other is the imponderables. This is a case of the imponderables. Every one of us, no matter how well we are loved, is subject to unknowns."

In later years Tom did commit a felony and went to prison where he bottomed out. Then he made a turnaround. Eventually, he began volunteering his time to offenders who ended up in trouble because of drugs and alcohol, the two habits that landed Tom in prison. He is restored and helping others. I am extremely proud of him.

What caused Tom to go to prison and then later become so important in the lives of others? The imponderables. But the imponderables, like Tom, are the exceptions. Perhaps as much as 85 percent of the time, crime involves the fatherless.

The greatest burden of all has been placed upon fathers. Without fathers for the youths of our country, how will we be able to reverse the vicious and deadly plague of crime in America? *

*In some of our large American cities murder claims nearly one citizen out of a thousand, while one out of thirty are victims of violent crime. Nationally, nearly one child in ten is exposed to domestic violence. These are average annual statistics. They do not include the much more prevalent property crimes and crimes of abuse (sexual, verbal, physical). One shudders to think what the actual statistics are for our unfortunate citizens living in crime-infested inner-city neighborhoods. (Statistics are from the 1996 FBI Uniform Crime Report and the 1994 ABA Report on the Impact of Domestic Violence on Children.)

8 People Change People

I leaned against the scarred pine waiting for Bill's recognizable stride to appear at the top of the hill. From a boy who didn't think his blood on snowy mittens was such a great thing—a kid who stuck with flag football mainly to please me, not knowing or caring for the most part which way we were running the ball; a youth who for years could not win a race—our son Bill was now within reach of becoming All-State. Win or lose, as I stood beneath that pine overlooking the three-quarter-mile marker, I knew I could never fault Bill for lack of heart or be prouder of his courageous accomplishment.

The late judge Paul Alexander of Toledo, Ohio, a great juvenile court jurist, displayed a sign in his courtroom. It read, "Attitudes are not changed by platitudes. Human conduct is changed by human contact. People change people."

In 1969 at Little Rock, Arkansas, I gained a new appreciation for these words.

Speaking before a group of citizens and professionals about the use of volunteers in court, my attention was drawn to a graying black man who sat in the first row. He seemed to glow—as if there were so much goodness in his soul a flimsy barrier of skin could not contain it. Love radiated from this man and reached out to me. Though he had not said one word all night, his presence dominated the room. One of the most Godly-appearing human beings I had ever seen, he fascinated me. I had to get to know him.

After completing my speech, I pressed through the crowd and introduced myself. His name was Luther Black. After a few minutes of polite exchanges, I said, "Mr. Black, I need a ride to the airport tomorrow morning. Could you possibly take me?" Luther said he would, and I asked if he could join me for breakfast, adding, "Luther, I usually like to have a big, leisurely breakfast, so could we meet early?" Truthfully, my normal habit is to gobble a little bread as I run out of the house, late as usual. But I needed to spend time with this man and discover what made him such a remarkable human being. With this ploy I managed to spend almost three hours with Luther Black.

At breakfast the next morning, we chatted for a while about the concept of Volunteers in Probation. Then I asked the question that was really burning in my heart and mind.

"Mr. Black, what makes you the person you are?" I figured that something extraordinary must have happened. Looking at Luther was like looking at the Grand Canyon. Its creation was not the accident of some pioneer stubbing his toe, nor the result of an Indian's kick at the dirt years ago. Rather, incredible forces worked wonders to create one of the world's most grandiose valleys. The same had to be true of Luther. He did not glow with such abundant love without having experienced a defining transformation.

Luther smiled. "Who am I and what am I? Why, what I

am goes back to my childhood. Though it was fifty years ago, I remember it like yesterday. I was the youngest of seventeen children on a sharecropper's farm in Arkansas. When I was eight my mother and father made two huge sacrifices so that I might go to school. First, they bought me some good clothes and shoes; and second, they decided they could get along without my help in the fields. I was the first one in the family to ever go to school.

"I remember that first day in school very well. I had never been separated from my brothers and sisters before, and I was terrified. To cover up my fear, I made noise. I tapped the chair in front of me and talked in a loud voice. I was very frightened, and the more frightened I became, the noisier I got.

"Suddenly, a huge figure loomed over me. I raised my head up slow and looked into the face of my teacher. She looked down at me without a smile, but with no meanness in her eyes. In a voice like a person would use for nighttime prayers, she said, 'Little Black, come with me to the front of the room.' She called me "Little Black" because I was the youngest member of the Black family.

"I dragged my feet, not wanting to follow. I just knew she was going to kick me out of school. What a disappointment I would be to my family. My dad would be very angry and spank me something awful when I got home.

"She interrupted my thoughts and fears as she sat down in her big chair and said, 'Little Black, read to me. Sit on my lap and read to me.'

"Still trembling, I sat on her lap and began to read. And as I read she gave me a hug. The more I read, the more she hugged me. She was a big woman. As I disappeared into her lap and bosom, my fear went away. I have never been afraid since.

"A few weeks later our class held a spelling bee, and I

85

reached the finals. They gave me a word—one of those with an *i* and an *e* in it. I didn't know then, and to this day I still can't remember which comes first. Is it *i* before *e* except after *c*, or *e* before *i* except before *c*—or what? I can't remember the rule.

"I shuffled my feet, stared at the floor, and was about to sit down in defeat when I heard my teacher clear her throat and cough. As I looked up she smiled, winked, and pointed at her eye. I knew the next letter had to be *i*. So I said the letter *i*, spelled the rest of the word, and won the contest. No one ever knew she had helped me. It remained our secret.

"That teacher gave me love when I needed it most. She knew, out of all the students in the classroom, that I needed victory the most. With so much against me, I needed a slight advantage. She bent the rules and helped me. That one victory gave me the boost I needed to achieve in school.

"Sometimes I think that's what love is about—helping someone achieve victory when he can't do it himself. And do it in secret so everyone else thinks he did it on his own.

"You know, she was the most important teacher I ever had, but I hardly remember a word she said. I guess what she taught me was important but not nearly so important as the fact that she loved me and helped me to get something I could not get by myself—victory and self-respect.

"I went on to the University of Arkansas, graduated, and completed post-graduate work at Columbia University. I later became the Director of Public Instruction, Adult Division, for the State of Arkansas. I have received many awards and honors. Plaques and certificates line the walls of my home. But the most important thing that ever happened to me was when my teacher put me on her lap and hugged me."

My time of sharing with Luther had a profound influence on my life. I learned a new appreciation for Judge Alexander's courtroom sign, especially the part, "People change people." I passed on Luther's compassionate testimony to Bill and our two other boys: If you want to change the attitude and conduct of the defendant who appears in court, you must wrap up love and concern for him in a person—one who cares, listens, loves, and gives of himself.

Luther Black summed up my life goals both as a judge and a father. I need to show my love for others, not merely talk about it. Talk is cheap and means little. Words have little impact unless they become flesh and blood in action. When I told our sons I loved them, were the words manifested in my life or were they empty words? The answer would validate my influence. Would I be regarded solely as their biological sire, or would I be esteemed as a nurturing mentor?

9  The Positive Influence of Others

The throng of slender, red-faced youths kept coming. *Ten...thirteen...sixteen...nineteen...there he is,* I silently moaned. My heart sank. He was running in twentieth place and laboring hard. He yearned for that All-State honor in spite of the odds against him. He must finish among the top fifteen of this race to realize his goal. Twentieth place was not good enough.

Now, Bill. You've got to make your move now. You can't do it later, I silently urged. As if he had heard me, Bill swung to the outside and spurted from twentieth to sixth place in less than a hundred yards.

"Go Ba-ee!" I yelled as he streaked by me. "Ba-ee"— our sentimental, perhaps even silly nickname for Bill had slipped out. When his younger brother Dave first started talking, he could not say "Billy." Ba-ee was the closest he could come, and over the years we used Ba-ee to lovingly tease Bill, though never outside our home.

When Bill was a toddler, we followed a nightly routine. The moment I arrived home he would drop his toy fire engine, blocks, or other playthings and run straight for me, jumping up and down and shouting, "Daddy, Daddy, you're home!"

He would put his tiny hand in mine and take me on an exciting journey through the backyard wilderness where imaginary rustlers, dragons, or monsters lurked behind every tree and shrub. After a meal in his fort, castle, covered wagon, or whatever shelter he pretended our house to be, we spent the rest of the evening playing, laughing, and enjoying each other.

Audrey shaped Bill's world during the day, but upon my arrival I became his world. I sometimes wished for a moment of privacy, but I loved every minute we spent together.

While watching the race I realized that Bill would soon leave for college, and our life together as we had known it would end. With amazing speed Audrey and I would be left with only our memories and the empty shell of his bedroom.

From the beginning I knew that perhaps my most important and difficult task was to prepare Bill for his departure and independence. A father should be the major inspiration in the life of his son for only so long. If Bill could not form meaningful relationships with others, if I did not strive to become unnecessary, I would have failed as a parent. What a joyful-sad realization of parenthood

The turning point of our relationship came when Bill entered junior high school. Audrey and I were concerned that he would withdraw in this large new school of 800 students. We encouraged Bill to form friendships by becoming involved in extracurricular activities—drama, sports, band, or French club. Probably to satisfy us more than himself, Bill tried out for football.

After his first day of practice, Bill ran into the house, bubbling with excitement, and told us about Mr. Conley, the young new coach from Iowa. "Mr. Conley said I ought to be able to make some touchdowns for the school!" Bill exclaimed. I had never seen him so enthusiastic. When it came to motivating kids, Jim Conley proved to be brilliant.

Jim's intense enthusiasm affected the entire student body. Over a hundred boys tried out for his team. He cut no one from the squad and played every member in every game.

I sought out and began to get to know the remarkable young coach who was an inspiration to so many boys. I learned that Jim had led a rough life as a younster. His father, an alcoholic, abandoned the family when Jim was a young child. Unable to care for him, his mother placed him in an orphanage. He never saw either parent again as a minor.

When he was thirteen the police caught Jim joy-riding in a stolen car. The owner, a Methodist minister, declined to prosecute. Instead, he asked the court if Jim could live with him. The court agreed. Through the minister's positive influence, Jim became an outstanding athlete, student, and law-abiding citizen.

Hearing his amazing story I asked Jim if he would consider working with ten difficult, hard-nosed young offenders —probationers of our court. Jim agreed and formed a group he called his "physical education class." For two hours each week they played basketball, volleyball, and other strenuous games. Afterward, as the ball lay inert, they worked mentally—sharing the feelings and problems that had caused them to lash out at society. As the group's one-year probation neared an end, I asked Jim how he was doing.

"Just great, Keith," he smiled, his square chin jutting forward. "These guys and I understand each other. You see, I was one of them when I was young."

Although the young offenders in Jim's group were among the most difficult cases passing through our court, none of them created further trouble with the law.

Jim often visited our home. While becoming a friend of the entire family, he became close-knit to Bill. He inspired Bill to play football beyond his capabilities. I believe Bill considered Jim Conley infallible. A man on that kind of pedestal can do much to help or hurt a vulnerable boy. Jim used his influence with care, and Bill benefited in many ways.

Jim Conley unveiled a paradox in my life. It pleased me that Bill had discovered inspiring qualities in another man. At the same time I felt disappointed—I was no longer the focus of Bill's world. Now I had to share the spotlight. The painful process of becoming unnecessary had begun.

When Bill entered the ninth grade, he changed schools. We were concerned about the detrimental effect this could have on his relationship with Jim. While talking with Jim I learned he was soon to be married and wanted to live in the country. My real estate partner, Van, and I had just bought a farm, so we invited Jim and his bride to live there and tend the crops. Jim eagerly accepted and invited Bill to work with him during summer vacations.

Jim and Bill's relationship thrived on that farm. For three summers Bill increased his physical strength by working in the hayfields. At the same time he grew in understanding and self-confidence by spending many hours of quality time with Jim.

We sold the farm during Bill's junior year because its size of operation was no longer economically feasible. It had more than served its purpose. Jim and Bill became lifelong friends, and Bill would draw upon Jim's influence athletically, academically, and personally throughout his life. Buying that farm turned out to be an investment, not in real estate, but in Bill.

Bill's heart and mind were also influenced by inspiring people who visited me professionally and often stayed in our home—Richard "The Lion-Hearted" Simmons of Seattle, Washington, for example.

A wisp of a man physically, with large, penetrating eyes flashing through black-framed glasses, Dick walks closer to God than any person I have known. My private name for him is "Ike," short for Isaiah, because being with this young minister is like walking with the ancient prophet.

In 1965, while deep in prayer, Dick felt called to restore the life of a forgotten man in prison. Dick asked the warden of the nearby maximum-security state prison for the name of a prisoner—one who had been there the longest and had received the least contact with the outside world by mail or visitors.

Dick began to visit "John," a bitter twenty-five-year-old who had served eight years of a long sentence for armed robbery. John's mother had died when he was eight. Throughout John's trouble-filled childhood, his alcoholic father had rejected and beaten him. During his time in prison, John received no visitors, no letters, and no birthday or Christmas cards.

At first John was surly and distrustful during their weekly two to three-hour visits. Dick expected this. One, two, three, then four months passed, and the hostile prisoner still would not accept Dick's love and friendship. Finally, in utter frustration, Dick wept in John's presence and agonized...*Why can't I convince the stooped figure with whom I share this depressing, six-by-nine-foot concrete and steel cage that I am here out of love? I am not here to study a psychological freak and write a book. Why can't I help this rejected human being?*

Suddenly, Dick lifted his face from his wet hands for he was no longer weeping alone. Both men in the cell were crying. "The Holy Spirit shook the hell in our hearts right out of our bodies," Dick told me later.

From that time on John opened up and looked forward to seeing his friend, Dick, each week. When John was paroled Dick met him at the gate, took him home for a meal, saw that he had a place to stay, and later helped him get a job. They kept in close touch. In time John adjusted to a steady job and a law-abiding life.

Dick's relationship with John spawned a network of programs variously referred to as "Job Therapy, Inc." or "Man-to-Man." Through these programs Dick and his associates have successfully matched more than seven thousand volunteers with thousands of hopeless, lonely, rejected prisoners.

Beginning in prison and continuing through the parole period or beyond, these dedicated volunteers do what one friend does for another. They listen with compassionate hearts. They counsel on family problems and pray for the future. They help in times of crisis. They refer prisoners to volunteer professionals who assess employment aptitudes. And they help find jobs.

"How desperate we are to have someone listen to us," a psychologist friend told me. "In former times people listened to each other. They sat on big open porches, in comfortable, quiet living rooms, on lawn chairs under big oak trees, and made time for listening.

"But now it seems as though we don't take the time to converse with each other. The truth is, most of us psychologists would be out of work if people would start communicating with each other again. People pay me one hundred dollars an hour just to listen to them. How desperate we are to have someone care enough to pay attention to us."

Dick Simmons and his peers do care. What does this

accomplish? Laymen and professionals working together as volunteers have greatly reduced the recidivism of thousands of hard-core offenders. In dollars spent by taxpayers alone, the savings comes to millions. In the quality of human life, the savings are beyond reckoning.

Another friend, Bob Moffitt, a former Peace Corps member with a perpetual smile, has introduced thousands of citizen volunteers into the lives of Denver, Colorado's, juvenile offenders.

When a Denver probation officer first meets a juvenile offender on probation, he asks him if he would like to join "Partners." Hostile to anyone in a position of authority, the young offender usually replies, "No. I don't want to join any club that you have anything to do with."

"Oh, I'm sorry to hear that," says the probation officer. He slowly and deliberately shuffles the Partner's application form and puts it back into his desk drawer. "I guess we'll just have to cancel that airplane ride and fishing trip we had set up for you."

"Wait a minute! What's with the big iron bird and the fish?" exclaims the juvenile as his hands grip the desktop.

"Well, that's part of the club," the probation officer explains, "but if you're not interested..."

"Wait a minute. Maybe I am," the youngster says anxiously.

The probation officer then explains that obligations and responsibilities go along with the fun. "You have to try to become a good citizen, try to commit no more crimes, and meet three hours a week with a citizen from the Denver area whom we select."

All his life the young juvenile has conned his way out of responsibilities; he figures he can handle the irksome stuff when it comes along. He'll join just for the initiation day—the airplane ride and the fishing—then he'll quit.

A few days later a middle-aged Senior Partner meets the new Junior Partner, and they ride with a Partners staff member to the airport. One of several private pilots who volunteer their time, talent, and planes, seats the youngster in the cockpit, takes off, and circles the greater Denver area for about thirty minutes. Often the pilot lets the Junior Partner manipulate the controls for a few seconds. The youth then comes back down to earth—physically, if not emotionally. Next, his Senior Partner whisks him away to a nearby trout farm. His hook, bare or baited, attracts dozens of fish. What a day of accomplishment for these otherwise non-achievers; they fly a plane and catch some fish!

A few days later the Senior Partner sends the probationer several pictures, a record of their first day together. Throughout the next twelve months the two Partners attend football games, roller-skate, and ski. More importantly, they talk and listen to each other.

Several times a year a hundred or more Senior and Junior Partners get together for group activities including skiing, tobogganing, mountain climbing, and rafting down the Green River. At the end of the twelve-month period, the young offenders are released from probation. Their cases rarely re-open. Steered away from a life of crime by someone who cares, these youngsters become productive citizens who make positive contributions to society.

Bob Moffitt told Bill and me about a frustrated Partners volunteer who once called him with a problem. "The school called and said my kid was cheating," the volunteer said dejectedly. "I'm really discouraged."

Bob responded with an enthusiastic, "That's great. Before you came into his life a few weeks ago that kid didn't care enough about school to cheat. Now he does. Don't you see what progress he's making? Now all we have to do is channel his desire to achieve into a willingness to study for his grades."

The volunteer rallied and continued the arduous process of changing a life. Like most of Bob's volunteers, he prevailed in an area fraught with perpetual failure.

Bob Moffitt has successfully matched hundreds of volunteers on a one-to-one basis in his Partners program. He, Bill, and I share another dynamic friend, Fred Ress.

Fred wears a streaming beard which is hard to distinguish from his long hair. As a college student and conscientious objector, he applied for alternative service rather than enter the armed forces. He was assigned to the Wilderness Canoe Base in northern Minnesota run by the Plymouth Youth Center, a division of the American Synod of the Lutheran Church.

I first became acquainted with Fred when I received an envelope from the Minneapolis based Youth Center in April, 1972. Inside was a formal proposal for funds that would enable Fred to combine juvenile offenders with kids who had not been in trouble. They would take wilderness canoe trips into northern Minnesota and Canada. His proposal intrigued me because I, too, had been working with young offenders. Besides, ten years earlier I had experienced the rugged canoe voyage from just north of Lake Superior to the James Bay area of Hudson Bay.

One of the statements in Fred's letter went to my heart: "The troubled youths will come back proud of what they have accomplished rather than ashamed of having been in jail or prison."

Proud of accomplishment rather than ashamed of failure—how simple and how true, I thought.

I immediately notified Fred that I would help obtain necessary funds, and I wanted to accompany him on one of his adventures. Four months later Fred, two court youngsters, a probation officer, my sons, and I hoisted canoes, packs, and other gear onto our backs and headed into the lush virgin pine forest north of Lake Superior near the Canadian border.

During our first night around the campfire, Fred told us about a trip he had taken the summer before. With a combination of imprisoned teenagers, straight kids, and kids who would most likely get into trouble in the future, Fred had paddled and portaged for seventy-three days from Lake Superior to Hudson Bay.

One of the imprisoned boys, "Ed," annoyed the others with noisy attempts to gain attention. The other boys ignored him. At one of the evening group discussions, each boy remarked that Ed was the last person he would want to be alone with on a trip.

"Why?" asked Fred as he glanced at Ed. Within earshot, Ed leaned against a tree. He seemed detached, nonchalant—as if he couldn't care less.

"Ed," they said, "is different. He doesn't want or need friends. He doesn't care whether people like him or not."

After they had talked this way for some time, Fred asked, "Isn't it possible that Ed wants and needs friends very much but doesn't know how to make them? Could he be trying so hard that he becomes obnoxious and turns people off?"

Everyone turned toward Ed and saw a tear-stained face glistening in the firelight. They realized what Fred said was true. From that night on Ed was one of them.

The straight kids came away deeply affected by the outdoor experience. One said, "Reform-school kids—horrors. Back home I wouldn't even talk to them, let alone associate with them. But out here we are forced to. We need each other. We may not get through the next rapids or portage if we can't get along with each other." This particular young man was surprised to discover that the reform-school boys were more sensitive to the needs of others, more responsive, and more perceptive about people than he was.

One longhaired, fuzz-faced boy—a deeply troubled sixteen-year-old—perhaps best described the effect of their wilderness experience. "Fred taught us how to love one another," he said. "On the trip he taught us that when you love someone and he loves you, you can hurt one another by your actions as well as unkind words."

Standing together at 3 a.m., our campfire sizzling and sputtering from a soft rain, my sons and I delighted in our new friendship with Fred Ress, a man committed to praising the Lord and loving kids.

Perhaps the most remarkable mutual friend Bill and I have is Walter Ungerer. Hard-working parents reared Walt in a cold-water flat of Brooklyn, New York. A tough kid, he became involved in street gangs at an early age, battling his way into gang leadership.

One night Walt, Bill, and I met together in our small redwood room. Walt, a burly man with a fearsome smallpox and knife-scarred face, told us about his former life. He and his gang often left bleeding comrades and rival gang members lying in the streets after their *rumbles*. He doesn't know if he mortally wounded anyone or not, but the possibility haunts his soul to this day.

With the temperature close to two hundred degrees Fahrenheit and sweat running down our faces, Walt told us how he and his gang were set to meet a cross-town rival. A big *rumble* was planned on that sultry summer evening long ago. There was little doubt that several kids, perhaps Walt himself, would die. But the other gang did not show up. Walt and his gang targeted their aggression onto several Presbyterians and Baptists preaching on a street corner.

The gang members laughed at, howled at, and shoved the lay preachers around. Walt grabbed a quiet, weak-looking young man by his lapels. The man looked right into Walt's eyes with compassion and conviction in his voice and said, "Christ loves you."

The words stabbed at Walt's heart. Never before had he thought anyone loved him. He let go of the man and slunk away.

Walt could not sleep that night. The layman's words raced through his mind as he repeatedly tossed and turned. Finally, in the tranquil predawn hours, he gave his life to Christ. He then miraculously escaped gang life. After a struggle to learn how to read, he completed college and divinity school and is now a minister.

Bill was deeply impressed with Walt, but then who wouldn't be, after hearing his incredible story?

When I consider how much these friends and others do for apprehended offenders, I savor the words of Dan Logan, founder of the "Y-Pals" volunteer program in Kansas City, Missouri: "I am only one. But I am one. I will not let what I cannot do prevent me from doing what I can do—to make this a better world, if only for one other person."

Some of the richest times in the sauna were those Bill and I spent alone. On one occasion I recounted my first Christmas away from home. I will never forget it: Anchorage, Alaska, 1944.

I was alone, serving in the military. During basic training and for some time thereafter, I had been stationed with a great bunch of guys. Unexpectedly, I was separated from them and sent to Anchorage a few days before Christmas.

I walked around the base on Christmas Eve, my mood matching the loneliness of the pitch-black night. As I looked up at the stars, however, they appeared to draw closer and glow brighter. I felt the presence of God. All of a sudden I had the urge to run. A Scripture verse came to mind, "They shall run and not be weary, they shall walk and not faint" (Isaiah 40:31).

If I had been running a race right then, I could have beaten anyone. It was twenty-five degrees below zero but I started to run. I wore army boots and a jacket. I became so hot I shed the jacket. I must have run five miles without getting tired.

I have never felt alone since then, even while stationed for the next eighteen months in the remote Aleutian Islands.

In the sauna I silently prayed that Bill would forever feel the sustaining presence of God and could run and not be weary. I was barely nineteen years old when I had my profound experience in the Frozen North—slightly older than our son who now, a generation later, was in the midst of his own defining race.

10 Between My Father and Me

My elation turned to anxiety as I watched Bill's figure head for the trees. Doubts flashed through my mind—and hopes. *Had he expended too much energy? With more than two miles to go, would he have enough strength to finish? He held sixth place. If he could maintain his position, he would fulfill his dream—All-State.*

We had discussed prayer and the power of God in relationship to running and decided Bill should not ask God for a victory. The other runners wanted victory just as much as he did. As in all the challenges we face in life, we knew we should pray for strength to do our best. If God's plan held victory, then we should use that victory for His glory. If His plan held defeat, we should use that defeat for His glory. We paraphrased Job 1:21 into our own verse: "The Lord gives victory. The Lord gives defeat. Blessed be the name of the Lord."

Suddenly, Bill stumbled and began to shake his right leg every time he raised it off the ground. *Oh no, what's wrong?* I wondered. My heart pounded in my ears as I strained to see what had happened to him.

There it was. A wood chip had stuck to the spikes of his right shoe, and Bill was desperately trying to shake it off, risking a pulled muscle or a fall. In his attempts to dislodge the chip, he drastically slowed his pace. The runners he had just passed were swiftly catching up.

In what seemed like an eternity, only twenty seconds passed; then the villain chip flew high into the air and came to rest beside the path. Bill resumed his normal pace and faded into the grove of trees. I knew I would not see him again for about five minutes while he ran the mile through the woods. I could only wait, hope, and wonder.

I recall the sheer pride that I felt in being the son of William Leenhouts. For a while he had to live and work in Detroit while my mother, sister, and I lived one hundred fifty miles away in Grand Rapids, Michigan. As soon as Dad drove into the driveway each Friday night, I would rush out and hand him a bat and ball. He had barely enough time to say hello to my mother and sister before my friends and I trotted out into the street where he hit the baseball to us. Other fathers on the block returned home every night. Yet mine was the first father to hit the ball to us since he had commuted to Detroit the Sunday before. All the kids waited for my dad to come home. When he drove around the corner, a cheer would go up. We were about to get the best fly balls since last Sunday. His popularity thrilled me, and I will never forget it.

Sometime ago I was in an eastern state helping a city begin a court volunteer program. The man who initiated the program had a sign on his office desk: "The most important gift a father can give to his children is to love their mother." Until that moment I do not think I fully realized the greatest gift my father gave to my sister and me. If any husband ever loved his wife, William James Leenhouts loved Dorothy Champion Leenhouts. They had a beautiful love affair. They sought common interests and pleasures. They were patient and kind to each other. They seldom argued.

Their marriage was a personification of the great love chapter of the Bible: 1 Corinthians 13...

"Love is patient and kind; love is not jealous or boastful; it is not arrogant or rude. Love does not insist on its own way; it is not irritable or resentful; it does not rejoice at wrong, but rejoices in the right. Love bears all things, believes all things, hopes all things, endures all things. Love never ends; ...So faith, hope, love abide, these three; but the greatest of these is love."

My dad cherished his wife. All he said and did mirrored his love for her. He was proud of her musical talents and would sit by the hour just to listen to her play the piano. He never appeared happier than when we had guests who loved to sing. Poor Dad, he couldn't carry a tune. His favorite joke about himself was, "I don't dare sing the national anthem. With my voice, it's treason." Nevertheless, he would sit admiringly and listen to the rest of us sing while Mother played.

After my mother's death I learned something else my father had granted her. A young policeman entered my office while I was a judge. "I just heard about your mother's death," he said with tears in his eyes, "And I'm very sorry.

"I had a miserable childhood," he began. "My father was an alcoholic. He and my mother separated. My mother had to work long hours to support us, and we didn't have much time with her. We were left to take care of ourselves.

"I think I could well have gone on to a life of crime and, in fact, did get into trouble. But when I was in third grade a wonderful lady began coming to our school and telling us stories from the Bible. She changed my life.

"Now I am a Christian as well as a policeman. I believe I can serve Christ better as a cop than in any other way. It was all because of that teacher I had in grade school, and that teacher was your mother. She gave me the greatest gift I have ever received in my life—Christ."

This was one of the proudest moments in my life. Listening to this police officer made me very appreciative of my mother. He was so young and strong, yet spoke with tears in his eyes.

After that I began considering my father in a new light. How many men of his generation would have encouraged their wives to enjoy full and abundant lives? He filled his heart with so much love and pride for her, there remained no room for possessiveness. The power of his love lifted my mother's life to its potential. As time passes I realize this more and more.

My father gave us another gift I did not fully comprehend until later in life. At the funeral home after Dad's death in 1955, I spoke with John Bosshard. While going to college I had worked with John during the summers. He told me, "You have something grand to look forward to. Until now you haven't been with your dad unless you were physically together. Now that's changed. The physical barriers have been removed. You can be with him all the time—spiritually. It'll take a while for the new relationship to begin—weeks maybe, months, or even a few years. When it comes, you will feel closer to him in a different way than before. You'll be together all the time."

Six months after my father's death, I discovered what John Bosshard meant. A new relationship was born. My father had lived his life in such a manner that he would never die in my heart. Love is immortal, and his love would be with me as long as I had life.

From that day until this, I have a definite awareness of

his influence upon my life—the things I do and my perspective on certain things. Could I live my life in such a way that my sons would experience my impact on their lives even after they laid me away in the grave? I hoped so. One of the goals of fatherhood is to live on in our offspring. Although attainable, our influence doesn't just happen by words. It happens by what we do and what we don't do.

Dad gave me another gift—the ability to see greatness in others and the desire to pattern my life after that greatness. Like everyone else, my father had weaknesses. Yet he did not build himself higher by dragging others down. He let my heroes be heroes: Lou Gehrig, Will Rogers, Charley Gerhringer, Joe Louis, Dutch Clark. They, too, were human beings with frailties. My dad never defamed them so that he might appear better. He didn't have to. A princely man doesn't have to knock others down to improve his own standing.

In seeking to persuade judges, probation officers, and wardens to use volunteers, I have to believe in people. But seeing goodness in others is not a universal attribute. This realization came to me during a trip to California.

"Joe" had worked with volunteers in our court in the early 1960's, then he moved to the West Coast. Early in 1967, when distrust of the volunteer concept still prevailed, he and I met with a group of professionals involved in courts and corrections. Few volunteers were being used anywhere in the country. California seemed the most suspicious and hostile state of all.

During our presentation in Los Angeles, we faced the coldest and least responsive audience ever. After the meeting a judge came to us unexpectedly and said he would give the concept a try. I reacted with a silent, *Thank you, God. Here is a judge who wants to help the offenders who appear before his court.*

As we left Joe confided in me, "I wonder what he wants. He is probably going to use volunteers because he wants to build up his reputation so he can get a promotion to a higher court. He might even want to become attorney general or governor."

Appalled at his viewpoint, I looked at him and said, "Joe, you know what's strange? That thought would never have occurred to me. This judge wants to help those he used to punish. I'm thrilled!"

After a moment of silence, Joe replied, "I'm sorry. It's my mother. She made me so suspicious of everyone. Because of her I can't think positive about anyone. I can't help but question the motivation of people."

Conversely, perhaps I am too trusting. I accept what people say at face value. Sometimes I end up disappointed— but to always question the motivation of everyone? What a way to live. Thankfully, my parents did not instill a suspicious nature in me.

I related this incident to another friend of mine, a man in his eighties who has learned much from life. He said, "You can tell more about the motivation of people by what they impute to others than any other way." When I thought about my experiences in California, this made sense. Joe would not merely help someone else; there would have to be something in it for him. With his distrustful spirit he could not believe someone else would do otherwise.

Years ago I heard a speaker say, "My father taught me never to love or trust anyone. 'Don't ever let anyone become a close friend,' he said. He told me that if anyone became close to me and I trusted him, he could swindle me out of my hard-earned money. So I followed his advice. I never trusted anyone, never loved anyone, and never had a friend. Now I am an old man, lonely and empty inside. My life has never been anything but drudgery. No one ever cheated me out of a dime. I have a lot of money now, and my dad always said that's important. Now I wish I had less money and at least one friend to love. I really have nothing of value."

My father, William Leenhouts, worked as a bank trust official. He spent much of his time helping veterans of World War I who had been emotionally and mentally damaged in battle. They needed someone to look after their interests. Dad administered trust funds for many veterans, and I became proud of this at an early age. To defend the defenseless, to help the helpless, to father the fatherless—I learned these were the noblest acts you could do. To be like my dad, someday in someway, became my goal.

My dad taught me another valuable lesson, one that I first experienced with the birth of my son Bill. Joy is found, not in the pursuit of pleasure, but in the fulfillment of duties. This may sound austere, but it proved true in his life and also in mine.

Golf provides an illustration. Dad took up golf before I was born. As I grew up he quit the game. His recreation turned to throwing the football to me, hitting fly balls to the neighborhood kids, enjoying athletic events together, and spending time with my sister and me. The golf bag collected more and more dust each year. He never played the game again.

I, too, played golf before our first child was born. When Bill turned three I put my clubs away. I didn't do it grudgingly or with a feeling of sacrifice; golf simply wasn't appropriate or enjoyable anymore. I didn't touch my clubs again until our son Dave started to play fifteen years later.

Deep and true happiness for me has never come through the pursuit of pleasures. Happiness has always been in the fulfillment of duties to others. Pleasure is diversion. True joy and happiness lie in fulfilling purposeful ministry and obligations.

My dad also endowed me with an intense interest in people. Whenever we went on a trip, we would stay at a tourist home. Often the rest of the family would go to a movie. Not Dad. He would sit on the porch and converse with the owner of the establishment. He listened with sincere attention and made other people feel important. He showed interest in them. He heightened the dignity of others by his real desire to learn from them and understand them.

Because of my father, when I read and heard that God was like a father, I wanted to be with God. If God was like a father, He was powerful, loving, good, and kind. He had to be, because that is exactly what my father was. I could sense God's power in him.

I know many who have drawn strength from the power of love—love of God, love of fellowman, love of parents for children, love of a man for his wife. Indeed, my mother tapped that source in her life and at her death.

I spent many nights at the hospital during the last three weeks of Mother's life. Cancer had ravaged the inside of her body. She was slipping fast. The early morning call came as no surprise. "You'd better come right away, Judge Leenhouts," the nurse said. "I'm afraid your mother's condition is rapidly declining."

When Audrey and I rushed into the sterile, pale green hospital room minutes later, Mother's thin white lips quivered into a weak smile. Through tremendous effort and love, she opened her eyes wide. Several times later during the day I suggested that she close her eyes and rest. But she would feebly shake her head, strain to open her eyes even wider, and murmur words I could not understand.

At two o'clock in the afternoon, Audrey and I decided I should leave to meet my sister flying in from Boston. When my sister and I returned from the airport two hours later, Audrey intercepted us in the hall. She told us, even as my departing footsteps still echoed in the hospital corridor, Mother closed her eyes and slipped into a deep coma. She had refused to go into that coma as long as her son was in the room.

We entered the room to the labored movement of our mother's chest and the raspy breathing—all that remained of her life. At five o'clock the nurse urged my sister and me to leave the room and get a sandwich. I raised my head from my folded hands and shook it.

Half an hour later the nurse again urged us to go, but we did not want to leave Mother. Finally, at six, both Audrey and the nurse urged us to go, and we reluctantly agreed. Later, they told us they could still hear our voices receding down the hall the moment our mother died.

Mother had fought her death until her daughter and son left the room. I was overwhelmed then and still am. Her love had literally reached back from the edge of the grave itself to bestow a final blessing on those she loved the most—sparing her children the sight of her death. This, her final gift, had come from the same source whence all her gifts had come: the awesome power of God's undying love.

11 The Awesome Power of Love

There was no way I could know how Bill was doing back in those woods. What other sport is there quite like this one? In football or baseball you don't lose sight of the players or the score during the game, but you do in cross-country. In spite of its irksome disregard for spectators, I still love the sport.

When Bill emerged at the two-mile mark, he could be first, last, or anywhere in between, or he might not come out of those woods at all. He could be limping along with a pulled muscle or bent over vomiting alongside the trail.

I ran, staggered, and walked with my fraternity of spectators to the two-mile mark, where we waited for the first runner to emerge from the trees. I visualized Bill as his spikes trampled the soft pine needles on the forest floor. I imagined the labored breathing and the incredible exertion he expended. He would be giving his all.

I remembered a story I had heard long ago—a touching account of father-son love.

A young man played, or should I say practiced football at an Ivy League university. "Jerry" wasn't skilled enough to play more than occasionally in the regular season games, but in four years this dedicated young man never missed a practice.

The coach, deeply impressed with Jerry's loyalty and dedication to the team, also marveled at his obvious devotion to his father. Several times the coach had seen Jerry and his visiting father laughing and talking as they walked arm in arm around the campus. But the coach had never met the father or talked with Jerry about him.

It happened during Jerry's senior year, a few nights before the most important game of the season—a traditional rivalry that matched Army-Navy, Georgia-Georgia Tech, or Michigan-Ohio State in intensity. The coach heard a knock on his door. Opening it, he saw the young man, his face full of sadness.

"Coach, my father just died," Jerry muttered with tears in his eyes. "Is it all right if I miss practice for a few days and go home?"

The coach said he was very sorry to hear the news and, of course, it was all right for him to go home. As Jerry thanked him and turned to leave, the coach added, "Please don't feel you have to return for next Saturday's game. You certainly are excused from that too." The youth nodded and left.

On Friday night, just hours before the big game, Jerry again stood in the coach's doorway. "Coach, I'm back," he said, "And I have a request. May I please start the game tomorrow?"

114

The coach tried to dissuade the youth from his plea in light of the importance of the game to the team, but Jerry persisted until the coach relented. Jerry could start the game.

Later that night the coach tossed and turned as he lay in bed thinking. *Why had he said yes to Jerry? The opposing team was favored to win by three touchdowns. He needed to play his best men for the entire game. What if the opening kickoff came to Jerry and he fumbled? Suppose he started the game and they lost by five or six touchdowns? What had he done?*

As the bands played and the crowd roared, Jerry stood at the goal line awaiting the opening kickoff. *The ball probably won't go to him anyway,* the coach thought to himself. *Then I can run one series of plays, making sure the other halfback and the fullback carry the ball, and take Jerry out of the game. That way I won't have to worry about a game-losing fumble.*

"Oh no!" The coach groaned as the opening kickoff floated end over end into Jerry's arms. Instead of fumbling, Jerry hugged the ball tightly, dodged three onrushing tacklers, and raced to midfield before he was brought down.

The coach was shocked. He had never seen Jerry run with such agility and power. Sensing something extraordinary taking place, he left Jerry in and had the quarterback call Jerry's play. The quarterback handed off, and Jerry responded by breaking tackles for a twenty-yard gain. A few plays later he carried the ball over the goal line for a touchdown. The other team was stunned. Who was this kid? He wasn't even in the scouting reports; up until then he had played a total of three minutes all year.

The coach left Jerry in for the entire first half on both offense and defense. Tackling, intercepting, and knocking down passes, blocking, running—he did it all.

At halftime the underdogs led by two touchdowns. As

for the astounded coach, in the words Carl Sandburg wrote of Lincoln, "Often with nothing to say, he said nothing." What wisdom in these few words.

During the second half Jerry continued to inspire the team. When the final gun sounded, his team had won. Afterward bedlam reigned in the locker room. The team had fought against impossible odds and triumphed. The coach sought out Jerry and found him sitting all alone, head in hands, in a far corner.

"Son, what happened out there?" the coach asked as he put his arm around him. "You've never played as well as you did tonight. You're just not that fast, not that strong or that skilled. What happened?"

Jerry looked up at the coach with tears in his eyes and said softly, "You see, coach, my father was blind. This is the first game he ever saw me play."

I like to tell this story in the sauna because you can't tell the tears from the sweat.

I remembered the time when I addressed our second national conference for volunteers in court and corrections programs. I wanted to tell the story of my mother's death but feared breaking down. As I took a walk early that morning, I met Bill Burnett, the first judge, as far as I knew, to use volunteers in a large city—Denver.

I told him my dilemma. He said, "I'll sit in the first row, Keith. If you falter I'll finish the story for you. But you won't. You can use my strength. I give it to you."

Several times during my speech, I began to choke up. But each time I looked at Bill and recovered. I drew upon his power.

When it was over Bill remained in his seat. I had never seen him so pale, drawn, and tired. Bill said, "I'm exhausted.

I can't get up." I had used up all his energy.

Only two courts that I knew of had made substantial use of volunteers by 1966—Royal Oak, Michigan, and Boulder, Colorado. A few others had tried the idea on a small scale, but it didn't last. Most cities thought the concept was absurd. "Volunteers?" they exclaimed, "They won't stick to it. They don't know as much as professionals."

As with everything else that is new, optimistic, and progressive, we heard the drone of thousands of cynics—those who said it can't be done.

I often traveled to other cities to promote the use of court volunteers. An unusual experience happened to me during a hectic trip to Texas.

The atmosphere in Houston was filled with pessimism, but there was also a stirring of positive response. A renowned American jurist, U.S. District Court Judge Woodrow Seals, and a few of his friends, invited me to speak before a large Methodist congregation.

The trip to Houston was physically, mentally, and emotionally exhausting. I spent the first afternoon speaking in Lubbock, Texas. Then I traveled to Houston. After that I spoke in Beaumont, Bryan, and Tyler, mostly to roomfuls of skeptics. My itinerary called for eight talks and meetings in four days. Because of my responsibilities as a judge, I left as late as possible on Friday and returned Tuesday evening.

I arrived in Houston on Saturday night. A group of five ministers and their wives met me. While we dined at a nice restaurant, they offered to drive me around Houston. I readily accepted. I like to see the history of an area through the eyes of locals.

As we got into the car, one of the ministers said, "By the way, Judge, your first sermon tomorrow will be televised, and you must speak for exactly twenty-two minutes. The second service won't be televised, so timing isn't a problem."

I was shocked. I hadn't known I was to appear on television. Furthermore, I had never timed my speech. I told my host I had better return to my motel instead of seeing the sights. I had a lot of preparation to do.

Alone in my room I timed my speech. Over twenty-five minutes. The content was good, but I had to cut three minutes. I tried a second time but still missed the mark. A third attempt also failed. I dropped to my knees and prayed in earnest, "Lord, if you want me to talk for twenty-two minutes tomorrow, you'll have to help me do it. I'm so tired I have to go to bed. If I don't get a good night's sleep, I won't be able to speak at all. It's up to you, Lord."

The alarm clock woke me from a restful sleep the next morning. I felt calm and peaceful as I rode to church. Thirty minutes later I entered the huge crowded church heated by bright television lights beaming from the balcony. After announcements, hymns, and prayers, I stood to talk. As I strode to the pulpit I knew, *"The whole world's in His hands."*

I felt like I was in a trance. The words I spoke could seemingly have come from any person in that room. The voice spoke for exactly twenty-two minutes. The second I stopped the television lights went out. The strength of God's love carried me through those twenty-two minutes.

The same power of love and faith helped me in a similar situation two years later. I was working at my desk in 1968 when the phone rang. An unfamiliar voice said, "Hello, Judge. My name is Rhett Maxwell, and I'm calling from Bethlehem, Pennsylvania. If possible we'd like to have you come to Bethlehem on the second Friday night and Saturday morning in December to help us start a volunteer program in our court."

I had never heard of Mr. Maxwell and explained to him that I avoided being away from home on weekends. I was willing to work sixty hours a week from Monday through Friday, but I devoted weekends to family, Sunday school, and church. I adhered to this self-imposed rule and violated it only about five times a year.

"But, Judge," Mr. Maxwell continued, "Please let me explain what's behind this call. Several months ago I read about Royal Oak's volunteer program in *Reader's Digest* and decided we needed a program like that in Bethlehem. I went to the court and tried to persuade the judge to begin a volunteer program. But he said, 'Mr. Maxwell, it's a crazy idea. I don't care what *Reader's Digest* says, I'm sure volunteers fail in Royal Oak and they'll fail here too. Please do us both a favor and forget it.'"

But Rhett Maxwell, an executive of Bethlehem Steel Corporation, is a Christ-centered man who does not discard promising ideas. He went home and thought and prayed. A few days later he returned to the court and sought out the judge.

"Judge," he began, "I understand you're a bit of a gambler. Well, I am too. I sometimes play golf for fifty cents a hole with my friends, just as you do. Every bid I make in business is a gamble. Now how about you and I betting on this volunteer program? Give me the worst, most hopeless young offender you have. Let me work with him for six months. If he doesn't improve in those six months, I'll get off your back and not bother you again. If he improves, you lose the bet and we start a volunteer program."

The judge laughed and said, "Okay, you have a bet. You can work with 'Luis,' a seventeen-year-old Puerto Rican. And believe me, Mr. Maxwell, Luis is a felony looking for a place to happen, and there's no way that you, I, or anyone else can help him."

Three months passed and Rhett grew depressed. Despite the intense love and concern he had shown daily to Luis, it looked as if Rhett would lose the bet—Luis wasn't responding. *Maybe I should stick to steel and forget the whole idea,* thought Rhett.

Rhett experienced the lesson every volunteer must learn. Sometimes the messenger overpowers the message. Who he is—a successful businessman or professional—may intimidate the unsuccessful probationer. He can't hear what the volunteer says. So, in spite of no apparent progress, the volunteer needs to persist.

An upcoming family vacation complicated matters. What should he do? Should he tell the judge he lost the bet and forget about Luis? Should he call and write Luis while gone? Or should he take Luis with him?

He and his family decided on the latter. For the first time in his life, Luis water-skied and swam in a lake. Most important, Luis witnessed genuine family love.

The experience deeply affected Luis. Toward the end of the six months, he found a steady job and married his high school sweetheart. Rhett and his family were the only non-Puerto Ricans at the wedding.

Rhett returned to the court shortly after the wedding and asked, "Well, Judge, did I win or lose?"

"I just can't believe it," the judge replied in amazement. "I've never lost a surer bet in my whole life, but I've never defaulted on a bet either. I won't begin now. You can start your volunteer program, and I'll cooperate in every way I can."

Relating this story to me over the phone, Rhett concluded, "Judge Leenhouts, I have been talking to the Lord and He says that you have to come here."

On the second Friday in December, I left for Bethlehem to meet with the city officials. I talked with them for three hours that night. Rhett gained their verbal commitment to start a volunteer program.

The next day I met with the one hundred and fifty citizens who would become Bethlehem's first court volunteers.

Rheet had personally telephoned every person in that room, urged each to attend, and repeated his conviction that something enormous was about to happen.

Except for the absence of a time limit, the situation reminded me of Houston. Again, the atmosphere scintillated with excitement. I felt as though I was in a trance. Anyone else in the room could have served as the spokesman. I acted as a vehicle for someone else's speech; I added nothing and took nothing away.

A standing ovation erupted when I finished talking. I stood still—drained and speechless. I could not even utter, "Thank you." As I looked at the audience standing and clapping, I could only think, *Lord, they are applauding You. I hope You are enjoying it.*

Then I noticed that many people—indeed most of them —were crying. So was I. But I wasn't ashamed of my tears for I remembered another line Carl Sandburg penned concerning Lincoln: "He was seen to weep in a way that made weeping appropriate, decent, majestic."

The city official who was supposed to acknowledge my address tried to do so, but he, too, was weeping. The words would not leave his mouth.

Bethlehem started its program. Rhett and the others poured their hearts into a tremendous amount of compassionate, intelligent work, which resulted in a very successful program.

12 The Finish

Suddenly, the first runner flashed between two tall pines that framed a final gateway out of the wooded maze. I could tell by the runner's stride that he was not Bill. Seconds later the next runner appeared—not Bill—too bent over. Bill runs straight up, probably too straight up. Another emerged from the trees; number three and still no Bill.

In an instant I saw him, running in a virtual tie with a youth who had beaten him by a wide margin all year. My heart pounded. Fourth and fifth place—either was All-State, Bill's dream. Pain, exertion, and intense desire contorted Bill's face. I had never seen him look so physically spent. To my worrying eyes, the other runner, younger and a grade behind Bill in school, appeared to run smoothly, relaxed, and with confidence.

I looked over at Bill's brother Dave who had joined me. No one ever had a more loyal supporter than Dave. Now our eyes met. We didn't have to say anything; both of us knew the elation we felt for Bill.

As I rushed along to the two-and-one-half-mile mark, I passed the start-finish line where Audrey stood. I saw worry in her eyes and knew she must be praying silently. Audrey had been an enthusiastic backer of everything Bill did: pouring out love and encouragement throughout the turmoil of

Bill's grade-school years, cheering at our flag football games, and attending Bill's track and cross-country meets.

Audrey and Bill had established a close relationship when Bill was young. I would hear her mother-talk: "Put on your boots." "Be sure to comb your hair." "Thank Mrs. Logan for the nice time." I think Bill understood that all of those words really meant, "I love you."

Bill and his brothers had developed a gentle way of telling her they didn't like something she had cooked for them. They would eat a few bites, then say, "Mom this sure is good ...but very filling."

Now as I ran past Audrey, she looked at me with hope and anxiety in her misty eyes.

"He's fourth!" I choked and turned away as tears clouded my own eyes. And I felt tired, so tired, propelling my legs on nerves alone, a lump forming in my throat.

The leader—a smooth, confident runner from Grosse Pointe—moved effortlessly past the two-and-one-half-mile marker. The second and third runners—also appearing to run easily without strain or pain—burst over the crest of the hill.

My eyes combed the hillside as I waited for Bill and the other youth who had battled so closely at the two-mile mark. The other runner appeared. *But where was Bill?* I wondered. *Had he tripped and fallen? The endless hours of running in summer and winter, the map on the basement wall—were they in vain? Would this be a final agonizing defeat?*

Then over the hill Bill appeared, running hard and straining every muscle. Tears rushed to cool my burning eyes as I saw Bill's sweat-and-spit-covered face—a runner needs to spit, but Bill said later that he didn't have time to turn his head. Fifth place and All-State lay 880 yards ahead.

I focused my attention for the first time on the runners behind Bill. Good. Only two were close. He should be able to hold on and finish within the top fifteen.

Gasping for breath I ran toward the finish chute, two 100-foot flag-marked ropes that narrowed to a V at the finish line. Everyone stood on the left of the chute, so I ducked under the ropes and dashed to an official's automobile parked on the other side.

I had just straightened up when the Grosse Pointe runner crossed the finish line to the cheers and applause of the spectators. What a great race he had run, finishing the grueling three-mile run in just under sixteen minutes!

Pressing against the ropes I kept my eyes on the course as the winner received his Number One card from the officials. The second and third runners, who had led Bill for the entire race, streaked through the chute. Their positions had not changed. What seemed an eternity passed before Bill and his close competitor entered the chute, numbly battling for fourth place over those last few yards. Both had given everything they had but were still matching each other stride for staggering stride.

Both runners crossed the finish line simultaneously. Overzealous officials, disputing who had finished fourth, grabbed their arms and roughly jerked the runners back and forth, trying to place them in official order. My face flushed with anger. It didn't matter if Bill was fourth or fifth—the race was over, and he had made All-State. Firmness was necessary, but the overreacting officials were throwing two exhausted runners around like police officers trying to break up a fight.

I looked at Bill's face. Agony twisted his boyish features as he staggered aimlessly down the chute. Thinking he was about to collapse, I quickly ducked under the ropes and ran to him. I grabbed his arm and put it over my shoulder.

Amid my ecstasy I felt a moment of alarm. Bill's reddened face was wet with sweat and spit; he rasped and gasped for breath uncontrollably as he staggered against me. I had never seen him so exhausted, so completely spent. His arm hung limp around my shoulder. For the few seconds we walked down the finishing chute, Bill leaned his weary frame on mine. He seemed nearly as helpless as the day we brought him home from the hospital nursery eighteen years before.

We must have been a strange sight shuffling down the chute—the spent runner clinging to a middle-aged man who was crying like a baby.

Abruptly, he straightened up and sighed deeply. "I'm okay now, Dad." He had recovered and was ready to jog a mile or so to cool down.

I was overwhelmed. I tried to hold back the tears that welled up in my eyes, but when I realized my efforts were futile I let the tears come. I tried to look at Bill but could not see him. I tried to talk but emotion quelled my voice.

I thought I would be prepared for this moment. But how could I have prepared for the overwhelming power of love? Father-son love. We were not celebrating the successful finish of a grueling race lasting a mere sixteen minutes. No. Much more had transpired here. We were celebrating a run of eighteen years duration—failure had been replaced by victory. My entire being cried out for the world to recognize how much I loved Bill, how proud I was of him, how defeat had finally succumbed to triumph. Love had conquered the impossible odds.

I turned away from the crowd and plodded step by step toward the woods where I sought solace. I walked cautiously—I could hardly see through the tears.

My innate sense of masculinity and toughness vanished. Those flowing tears gushed forth from a well of spent emotions. For me to become so overwhelmed something remarkable must have happened. Indeed it had. For deep in my heart I knew I wept in a way that made weeping appropriate...decent ...yes, one might even say...majestic.

 Epilogue

Bill Leenhouts was awarded fourth place in the 1972 Michigan All-State Cross-Country Race, thereby achieving his long-sought goal of All-State. After high school he attended Central Michigan University. He graduated in 1977 majoring in teaching and physical education. Although he competed in track and cross-country for two years, his college courses proved too demanding to allow both sports and studies. He abandoned his dream of competitive running at the national level, choosing, rather, to dedicate his time and energy to obtaining an education.

Bill has remained single and teaches physical education at a grade school in Hazel Park, Michigan. For many years he was an instrumental leader in a Christian Camp ministry for Detroit's troubled youths.

The book you now hold in your hands has quite a history. The author, Keith Leenhouts, and his wife, Audrey, have three sons. Each son was presented with a book on the Christmas following his high school graduation.

Bill's book was entitled A Father...A Son...And a Three-Mile Run. It was written in 1973, published in 1975, republished in 1984 and again in 1999. Approximately 120,000 copies of the book were printed, including the popular

English version plus five other languages through 1984. In October, 1974, *Reader's Digest* published an excerpted version entitled, *"Race for Love."* A movie based on the book was made in 1983 by Ken Heckmann and distributed by Evangelical Films.

The books written for sons Dave and Jim Leenhouts also focused on their individual lives and relationships with family and friends. Both sons are married and are active Christians in the suburbs of Detroit. Dave is a minister with the United Methodist church.

Keith and Audrey look forward to their golden wedding anniversary in 2003. They enjoy a fulfilling family life, complete with delightful grandchildren.

Keith Leenhouts continues to teach Sunday School, and write and speak on behalf of Volunteers in Probation. His current focus concerns Christian involvement with the courts, which is discoursed in his latest book, *Crime, Courts and Christ.* Copies are available from Keith Leenhouts at 830 Normandy, Royal Oak, MI 48073.

The publishers welcome your comments or inquiries regarding *Father, Son, 3-Mile Run.* Correspondence may be directed as follows:

Clearwood Publishers
P.O. Box 52
Bella Vista, CA 96008
Fax: 530-549-4598
e-mail: clrwood@c-zone.net

Website: http://www.c-zone.net/clrwood